What More Is There to Say?

Stories of a Very Good Life

Elaine Colton

Author of *The Newport Girls*

What More Is There to Say?

Stories of a Very Good Life

Elaine Colton

WHAT MORE IS THERE TO SAY?
STORIES OF A VERY GOOD LIFE

iUniverse books may be ordered through booksellers or by contacting:

iUniverse
1663 Liberty Drive
Bloomington, IN 47403
www.iuniverse.com
1-800-Authors (1-800-288-4677)

Because of the dynamic nature of the Internet, any web addresses or links contained in this book may have changed since publication and may no longer be valid. The views expressed in this work are solely those of the author and do not necessarily reflect the views of the publisher, and the publisher hereby disclaims any responsibility for them.

Any people depicted in stock imagery provided by Thinkstock are models, and such images are being used for illustrative purposes only. Certain stock imagery © Thinkstock.

ISBN: 978-1-5320-0846-7 (sc)
ISBN: 978-1-5320-0847-4 (e)

Library of Congress Control Number: 2016919145

Print information available on the last page.

iUniverse rev. date: 12/05/2016

For Todd and Jim

The best sons a mother could have

Contents

Prologue

I've noticed that when you get to a certain point in life not only do you appreciate the joy of the present, but you also conjure up lots of memories from the past. For this book I have chosen those stories that were not only memorable but also put a smile on my face. I acknowledge that sometimes they were tough and other times...well, I just say, "WOW, did I have that much chutzpah?" They begin in my teenage years and continue into today (2016).

I hope this ride down my memory lane will spur some inspiration followed by action.

There is no such thing as failure when it comes to writing stories of a very good life. Be bold. Go for it. Be adventurous. Dare to create something. Have fun.

The context of one's life starts at the beginning, and mine was pretty much uneventful until the age of nine in 1950. Harry

F. Truman was President. My mother was taken away. She was mentally ill and it was quite a traumatic time in my life. That trauma ended when I met Arlene Callahan; we were both eleven. We lived across the street from each other. We became inseparable for the next seven years while we lived in Rhode Island and are still best of friends sixty-four years later, as we live our retirement years just twenty-five miles apart in Southeastern North Carolina. We've had many adventures as chronicled in my book, *The Newport Girls.* This story begins in our teenage years.

At the end of my life I want the experience to be that I've been all used up. How glorious-a life well lived.

Falling into an Ice Cream Freezer Case and Appendicitis

In 1958 Alaska and Hawaii became the 49th and 50th states, respectively, of the United States.

It was sometime in that year that I had been having stomach pains. However, that slight annoyance did not keep me from putting on my illustrious light green polyester uniform and having my father drive me to my night shift at the Newport Creamery in Middletown, RI. Now one might ask, "Why doesn't she drive herself to work; after all, she is 17?" Only someone who knew how my father's brain worked would know his logic deduced that all my friends had their driver's licenses; therefore, I didn't need mine. GO FIGURE!

I had a great deal of pride in my job as an ice cream scooper and took it very seriously and went to work with my usual bubbling personality, but now, in pain. As the evening went on and customers came and went, the pain increased and only after I doubled over and fell into an ice cream tub while scooping did I begin to realize it might be a good idea to go home and have this checked out. When I got home, I begged my dad to go get me some Milk of Magnesia so I could literally eliminate the pain. However, that was the worst thing I could have taken.

It didn't work and after a very quick visit from our family doctor and a rush to Newport Hospital, my appendix, in all its glory, as well as some other body organs, were removed from my teenage body. Unbeknownst to me, I had been a very sick girl. I think I forgot to mention that I'd walked around in this condition for an entire week before I took the whole thing seriously. When I awoke the next morning, after surgery, there was a priest at the end of my hospital bed praying. *Very strange,* I thought. *I'm Jewish.* It wasn't until the doctor explained how serious all this was that I appreciated the prayers. Apparently my appendix had been burst for some time and what I had thought was an upset stomach had been a ruptured organ wreaking havoc on other things. Peritonitis had set in, forcing half of my bowel to be removed. Had I been ten years older, I would have likely died, but my teenage strength and condition saved my life. Who cares if one has a six inch abdominal scar?

The doctor did apologize for having to cut so much, but years later that scar just blended in so nicely with my stretch marks. I truly appreciate the priest, whoever he was. Needless to say after fifty-plus years, I still have stomach issues, BUT I'm alive. No whining!

The Drive-in and the Pizza Night Adventure

After I healed from my appendicitis attack, and having driven my family crazy with my boredom, my father let me go to New York with some girlfriends and on my return, I had a pajama party (I think these days they are called sleepovers).

From age fifteen, I'd worked at the Newport Drive-in, graduating from ticket taker to concession girl. I really loved the promotion as I got to be inside, no matter what the weather, and I could still watch the movie before and after my intermission duties.

Back to the PJ party. Like most girls, we hardly ever slept at these things and in this instance I had a hand up over most of our group, because I had the backup of the Drive-in. As we got rowdier and louder I suggested we grab our blankets, sneak out, walk over to the Drive-in, wake the owners and get them to make us pizza. Their names were Ike and Zeke, and they often stayed over rather than drive home to Fall River, MA. I knew they were there that night. At about 1:00 or 2:00 am the group of us (maybe 8 or more) traipsed out of my house and in the dark of early morning left my neighborhood. It must have been somewhere around a quarter mile or so: not that it was far, but we were in total darkness. It never occurred to us what someone might think if they approached us in a car-a gang of girls walking across a main road and going into a dark Drive- in theater. Well, did we care? Hell no.

We got to the very back door and started banging and yelling their names. After several minutes a very groggy Ike turned on the lights to see who the hell had interrupted his sleep in the middle of the night. He was hardly amused at the smiling faces that met him behind the glass door, but in spite of himself, he opened the door, because of course, he recognized me. After he was somewhat awake and really heard our request, he woke Zeke and asked him to join in making pizzas for us. Not only did they make us three pizzas and didn't charge us (like we had any money in the first place), but we all sat around and laughed and ate together. After we were stuffed, we hugged said "thank you" and trotted back to my house. It had been a very special party indeed. How great were these guys, anyway?! And pizza-well, at any hour it is always a treat.

The Liverwurst and Grilled Cheese Sandwich Invention

My Newport Creamery days were not over yet, but I did now have the opportunity of working the day shift. I can't remember how I got to work-maybe the bus-but I did and it was a joy to serve daytime patrons. We had a very extensive lunch menu and I became very proficient at making burgers on the grill.

After a while I had learned to make (and eat) everything our menu had to offer. One of the perks of this job was that on our 30-minute break we could eat whatever we wanted. Naturally, being the carnivore that I am, I did rare burgers every which way I could imagine and then I graduated to the regular sandwich fare. The truth be told, I am less excited about tuna fish on rye than I am about grilled cheese. The Creamery, to this day, has the best relish I have ever tasted. I put it on everything. On grilled cheese it truly is delish. I thought that I'd exhausted every good idea I had when it came to me: there was one thing

I had not concocted yet. In fact it was so bizarre to me I wasn't even sure I'd do it, but lo and behold, my greatest masterpiece was created: the LIVERWURST and GRILLED CHEESE with relish sandwich was born. No kidding, it was so fantastic (to my palate) that it trumped anything I had ever made. I felt like Julia Child creating a new way to prepare chicken. To this day, because I ended up substituting honey Dijon mustard for relish, it is one of my prize recipes (I don't cook).

Before the Airlines

The year was 1959 and John F. Kennedy was to become our president. After the Newport Creamery, I finally had a plan for my future (so I thought). Off to Boston I went at age eighteen and a half to wait out my time until I was twenty. That's the age that I could apply to the airlines to become a stewardess. I had no real skills other than "people" skills: I was great at serving folks, being funny and friendly, and I thought I was somewhat brave. Honesty was right up there as well. The honesty paid off leading up to my airline days.

Here's the scoop on that.

I had a plan when I got to Boston. I would go to Bonwit Teller (the most exclusive ladies' store at that time) and get a job until I was old enough to interview with the airlines. I would then interview with every airline I could get an appointment with and the first one that would hire me-well, you get the picture.

The hiring folks at Bonwit's were very professional and much older than I. Part of their curiosity was related to my age. The question went something like this: "Miss Glickman (my maiden name), why would you like to work at Bonwit Teller? After all, you would be our youngest employee." My answer was so simple, because it was true. "I want to work at a very exclusive store until I'm old enough to apply to the airlines to become a stewardess. That would be a little shy of one and a half years that I'd be an employee here," I answered. As I recall (and remember, this is going back some fifty-five-plus years ago), they hired me on the spot, saying they had never had such an honest future employee. They also said they'd not only be pleased to have me but when the time came they'd allow me all the interview time I needed to meet with the airlines.

I couldn't have been happier, as I knew that the airlines were very strict about your time between high school and the time you applied to them. As my college life had been extremely short-lived, I chose to not put it on my application and went right from high school to Bonwit's and that ultimately did the trick. My days at Bonwit's were just wonderful. Everyone who worked there embraced me because, as it turned out, I was the youngest employee the store had ever had. On top of that, I was assigned to the robe department.

Everyone who worked in that department was forty-plus years older than I. I got a lot of mothering. I didn't mind at all. Mostly very older people bought robes and bed jackets (as they were called) and I really needed major coaching on how to serve these women. That coaching came in very handy during my airline year.

The year was 1960 and I was just shy of my twentieth birthday. We had severed our relations with Cuba and I applied to all the airlines where I thought I might have a chance of being hired. I self-edited my choices since I knew the requirements of them all. Any airline that flew beyond the United States required an ability to speak another language as well as some college. The language part eliminated some, as well as the college requirement. Having excluded several (there were fewer airlines back in 1960 than there are today) I applied to Eastern Airlines (no longer in existence) and American. Both of these accepted my applications and I flew to Florida to interview with Eastern and was lucky enough to meet with the American representative in Boston. Lucky for me, American hired me and in January of 1961, I flew to Ft. Worth, Texas to begin AA Stewardess School.

Before I left Bonwit Teller, the executives were kind enough to say they had appreciated my loyalty and honesty while I worked there. It was a very good way to leave and gave me the freedom to begin the next adventure of my life with integrity.

Airline Adventures

Let me start out by saying that everything at American Airlines Stewardess School was beyond amazing. The school was opened in 1957 when the Soviets started the space race by launching Sputnik, the first unmanned space ship. The AA facility was the first school dedicated to the profession of stewardesses. AA was in the forefront of everything in 1957, so when I attended in 1961, I really was somewhat of a pioneer. According to Millie Alford, the head of the school at that time and one of the first AA stewardesses, each one of us (our class) was one out of five hundred women who had applied for our job. Apparently, we all fit the mold of the typical all-American girl. The training was quite intense, with the primary focus on safety. We had to learn every piece of emergency equipment on every type of aircraft that AA flew. The people part of training included greeting passengers, food service and our cordiality. The tests were grueling and there could be no score below ninety-five percent or you were out. I'm not sure, but I would think today's requirements would be even more stringent than those of fifty-four years ago, considering the possibilities of some act of terrorism, whether homegrown or foreign. After graduation I was assigned to Boston as my base. I was thrilled because I could take the "T" (the subway) all the way from the city to the airport.

We deadheaded (flying free until we got bumped by a paying customer) and upon arriving in Boston, I was assigned my first flight to San Francisco the next day. With barely any sleep, I arrived at Logan Airport somewhat nervous, excited, and sleepy. Let me tell you though, when you left stewardess school you felt like you were the luckiest and most capable girl in the world, and for six hours that day I muddled through my first flight. Let's put it this way: getting your driver's license doesn't necessarily mean you're a great driver: that takes practice. It's the same with being a great stewardess: that takes practice too. By the time my career had concluded due to marriage I had become a pretty good stewardess, if I do say so myself.

I had some very funny (and some not quite so much) experiences in my airline days and some come easily back to memory.

In those days, because I was so junior to most of the other women at my base, I worked mostly the three-day trips from Boston to Cincinnati and back. These were mostly on DC6s (four engine planes) that held about fifty eight passengers. There were three crew in the cockpit and two stewardesses in the cabin. On the first leg of that flight we made nine stops between Boston and Cincinnati, ending up in Irvington,

KY (where the Cincinnati airport is). We were given a flight manifesto with the names of each of our stops, along with the names of prominent people who were flying with us. The purpose was to cross out the city we had just come from and welcome the boarding passengers according to where we were. We also called several passengers by name on each flight. Nine stops in and out meant nine takeoffs and nine landings. Need I say more? A very long day.

Three very funny things, according to me, happened on that first ninestop flight. The first was that I was flying SENIOR to the other girl, which meant she had graduated from stewardess school one week after me, which meant I took the lead: announcements on the PA system, bringing coffee to the crew, ticking off our stops correctly and welcoming the passengers. That was almost like the blind leading the blind, but nothing like being thrown to the lions and coming out alive (that might be a little dramatic), but that's how it felt!! So I put on a perfect low PA voice and welcomed the passengers from Boston to Cincinnati with nine stops. Everyone was in his or her seat, under his or her seatbelts and everything was going well. We had made about four stops into our flight and as we taxied out from the gate to the runway, just about to take off for stop number five, I welcomed our recently boarded passengers to flight #? (Whatever it was), by saying, "I'd like to welcome our onboarding flyers to Cincinnati, with stops in (blah, blah, blah). Our next stop is Rochester." Well…there were about eight or nine different voices saying, "Am I on the right plane?" I then looked down at my paper and realized our next stop was Syracuse. I had forgotten to cross out a city where we'd already been and I had totally messed up our stops. I quickly said into the microphone, "OOPS!!! How about our next stop is Syracuse?" and everyone applauded.

The rest of that flight was quite uneventful until our next to the final stop. We (the other stew and I) had fifty six minutes, takeoff to landing, to serve fifty eight passengers a meal; NO KIDDING. That included beverages on their dinner trays. We hardly breathed as we ran back and forth in our aprons and flat shoes dispersing trays. After all the trays were out we served coffee and then began collecting trays to get them back into the containers before the plane started its descent. As we were practically sprinting up and down the aisle, a gentleman stopped me and said, "Excuse me, Miss, might I have a cup of tea?" I think I looked at him and said something like, "You're kidding, right? We'll be on the ground in less than ten minutes and I'm sure you can have a nice cup when you get home." In retrospect I can't believe I said it-how rude was I? On the other hand, my twenty year old trained self could not believe he asked. We landed with no further incidents.

This would be the time to tell you about the glamour of being an airline stewardess but there's not much. I'm only talking about my experience. I wasn't there long enough to enjoy the perks of travel, so my point of view is quite narrow. For instance, I saw the inside of hotels (the same ones week after week, since I always flew the same route). The only time I didn't stay in a hotel was when, on rare occasions, I flew Boston to

LaGuardia to Hartford, to LaGuardia to Hartford, Hartford to LaGuardia, LaGuardia to Hartford, to LaGuardia and back to Boston. Those flights were quite grueling and when I returned home, all I wanted to see was my bed!!

Motel or hotel beds were just for sleeping because after a trip, all I wanted to do was sleep. I don't ever think I got used to the long scheduled days. Although I truly loved flying, I think I ran on adrenaline most of the time. Back to the three day trip. Day two was ONLY Cincinnati to Cleveland with a day layover before we made our nine stop trip back to Boston. Three days "on" then two days "off; just enough time to wash your clothes, have a little social life and then back to the plane.

The next story is a little more interesting than the "tea event." On our nine stop trip to Cincinnati we were about to start our descent when I heard four bells: ding, ding, ding, and ding. No crewmember ever hit four dings: usually two dings for coffee. That's all we ever heard from the cockpit. This was an emergency. I quickly, but with resolve, went to the cockpit to discover that the captain was not able to get our landing wheels down and he asked me to prepare the cabin for an emergency landing. Believe me, no one ever thinks this is going to happen, but my training kicked right in and after telling the other stewardess what was happening, I got on the PA and asked everyone to prepare for a challenging landing. Amazingly, no one panicked and we walked through the cabin and showed people the correct position for a difficult landing, asking each one to remove glasses, contacts, false teeth and any potentially dangerous items: keys, pens, etc. Surprising as it was, the captain finally got the gear down and we avoided a crash; not one passenger was any the wiser. When we landed we ushered all the passengers off, explaining that we had a mechanical issue with the plane and they would be taken care of by ground staff to make sure they would get on the next available flight to reach their final destination. One's fright is totally contained when a situation like this occurs, because all you think about is passenger safety (as well as us and the crew) but when the last passenger deplaned I totally "lost it" for both fear of what might have happened and gratitude for it not happening.

At that time, American's primary repair facility was in Tulsa, OK. The captain contacted them and was immediately told to ferry (fly with no passengers) the plane there, to undergo a complete mechanical inspection and to perform anything necessary to correct the landing gear, and look for other issues that might need attention. At that point the captain asked us if we wanted to fly to Tulsa and then get back to Boston by deadheading on the first available flight. We said, "Yes," of course and we had the most unbelievable experience flying in a big plane with only the five of us. AWESOME!!!!

PS: The Douglas DC6 airplane was first ordered by American Airlines in 1946 (the year that Dolly Parton was born), could fly at an altitude of 28,000 feet, had four 2,400-horse power engines and could attain a speed of 308 mph. It was a true workhorse and could travel almost 3000 miles at one time.

My next experience, somewhat dramatic (but also somewhat funny), took place on our way to LaGuardia from Boston, one of those one day back-and-forth trips to Hartford that took all day. As we were flying along I noticed that it suddenly got a little quieter in the cabin. I looked out the right side of the plane to see that one engine had STOPPED. The good thing about a DC6 at the time, was they were rather noisy. In other words, you could hear the engines. Passengers and crew got used to the noise, so when one engine stopped the noise adjustment was quite minimal. I started closing window shades so no one would see and get nervous. It was a very light and quick flight so the other stewardess and I decided we'd serenade the guests and ask them to join in as well. Although this was not routine, folks started singing along until we prepared for landing. As the passengers left the plane they all thanked us for an unusual but delightful trip. We beamed from ear to ear and that day-no kidding; I really realized how truly safe a DC6 was. I had more respect for it, and never longed to work 747s again. Good thing, because it was the DC6 until the end of my career.

Then there was the time we got another four dings from the cockpit while we were on the runway, about to take off. The captain made an announcement that we were returning to the gate, as something was wrong with the instrument panel. No panic, just annoyance from the passengers as they all got off and returned to the airport to handle getting rescheduled for another flight. We knew the real reason we had aborted our takeoff: a bomb threat had been called into the airline, and all I can say is how relieved I was that we hadn't been up in the air when we found out. The bomb-sniffing dogs started doing their thing in the cabin, cockpit, luggage compartment, and the complete outside of the plane. Thank goodness they found NOTHING. We were escorted to another plane to take over the scheduled flight and an hour later we took off with no incidents. We all were quite happy. It was a very boring flight (just the way we liked them).

This final tale has to do with the resilience of my 20 year old constitution. It was about an hour into a several hour flight (to where, I can't remember) when all of a sudden we girls noticed it was beginning to get very warm in the cabin. The captain came on the PA to say that we were perfectly safe but the circulating air had stopped and that he would land the plane as soon as we were cleared into the nearest airport. Not a problem for me, but the passengers, well that was another story all together. Every person began removing as much clothing as conventional modesty would allow, and one by one they grabbed for the "barf bag" and we could not get to people fast enough before they needed another one. The other stewardess also got sick and I was running all over the cabin by myself and tried to replenish those damn bags before another accident happened. Let me say that the air never circulated before we landed somewhere. Passengers required lots of assistance from the plane and the cabin cleanup crew had a Herculean job that day: you get the picture!!

Other than these incidents that I can recall, I truly loved my job and was sorry I had to leave when I got married. In those days there was no flight attendant union. The rules changed later, and for those who still fly, I'm sure you've noticed that many people continue to work flights well into their middle age; in fact, according to AARP the oldest flight attendant retired from United Airlines at age eighty three, after flying for sixty three years-an industry record. An American Airlines flight attendant, as reported by AARP, had flown for American Airlines for fifty-three years-a record for AA. I really don't think I would have wanted to fly that long (smile!!)

Postscript to these stories about my airline days:

Back in 1946 American Airlines stewardesses created an organization of former AA stewardesses where they could socialize, reminisce and in the future become a charitable organization. They called themselves The Kiwis, after the wingless bird from Australia. After I departed from flying and after several years of being involved with the Boston Chapter, I became its president in 1967-8. Since so many years have passed since my involvement, I researched the club and discovered the following facts:

Millie Alford, one of the first stewardesses to fly the AA skies and the woman who ran our Ft. Worth training facility, was given lifetime membership at a National Convention. Also, at the 31st Convention in Las Vegas in 2014, all the flight attendants who flew on AA Flight #11 and AA Flight #77 on

September 11, 2001 were given honorary membership status. Theirs had been an enormous sacrifice.

I will always be honored at being worthy of being an American Airline stewardess in 1960 and a KIWI forever.

The Wayland Town Crier

Circumstances after my divorce forced me back into the job market. It had been eight years since I left the airlines and even though I still qualified to fly, I knew it wasn't the right thing to do, as I had two small children to care for. Hardly being up on the job market, I took the path of least resistance and applied to our local weekly newspaper for a position in sales. Not having formal training in sales, I hoped my time at Bonwit Teller and being a former stewardess would be enough to qualify me for a job; and it was. I interviewed with the sales manager and the publisher (both really great gentlemen) of our town weekly periodical, and when the sales manager asked me why he should hire me, I did not hesitate for one second when I answered, "Well, if you don't hire me -, no problem, I'll just go down the street and apply at another paper." I guess he took me seriously and hired me.

The several years that I worked at the Town Crier were just wonderful. I can't remember the circumstances of how my children were taken care of in those days, but I knew they were, which allowed me to do my job with no concern for their wellbeing during my workday. That lack of worry gave me the opportunity to do a very good job. I was assigned the position of real estate salesperson, which required calling on the usual real estate firms in our area that already advertised in the paper. All of them were already running ads weekly with additions of new properties for sale, and the deletion of some that might have been sold. Week after week I collected their ads and photos of their featured homes and the night that we "put the paper to bed," prior to going to the printer, I would work with the production team laying out the Real Estate section of the paper. It usually was four or five pages long and was at the very end of the paper, which meant that every week I had to sell the back page.

Moving Back into the School District

A brief story inside my days at the Town Crier:

My oldest son was in first grade at a great elementary school right at the end of our street. He was very happy there and was doing quite well. One day I got a notice from the school that they were removing our street from the school district and would now require my child to ride a bus to another school. This being totally unacceptable to me, I jumped into action and contacted the school department to request a face-to-face meeting with the school board. For some reason they granted me one, and at the meeting I proceeded to explain to them all the reasons I was against this upcoming redistricting. The day of the meeting I was quite determined to get my point across. They all listened politely and then told me that issue was all ready to go forth as planned and they were sorry that they couldn't accommodate me.

Undeterred, but somewhat annoyed, I decided to make a move back into our school district so my son could continue at his school. Ironically, the move only required us to move six blocks from where we were currently living and though it was financially challenging, my kid was more important. We moved on a weekend and he never missed a day of school because of all this.

The Town Crier continued...

Lucky for me, there was always someone who wanted to buy the back page space and I helped with the revenue growth. Every week there was always a "special opportunity" to buy another full page in the paper and most weeks I could sell it. I was a very good newspaper salesperson and was learning so much along the way. I made some wonderful friendships with people who worked in the real estate industry and they always acknowledged me for doing such a good job with their ads. I was very appreciative of having had that job, and when the opportunity came along to join a newly formed local paper elsewhere, I did, with a somewhat mixed feeling of sadness at leaving and on the other hand, excitement at being part of something brand new.

The Paper

I was hired as the production manager for this new tabloid called The Paper. I thoroughly enjoyed putting an entire newspaper together with the editor each week. That job was going quite well when one day, out of the blue, the publisher called us all into the large production area and told us he was closing down The Paper. Without a doubt we were all stunned, because we had only been up and running for a little over a year. We all guessed that it just wasn't cost effective to have another weekly compete with those already in place. We asked when this was going to take place and were told "TODAY." In disbelief we all cleaned out our desks and headed out, in a caravan of cars, to the nearest unemployment office. The publisher must have called ahead to say "X" number of people were on their way, but when we arrived the staff was totally overwhelmed. Did I tell you that my sales manager from the Town Crier had also left to become the new sales director of The Paper? We were in the same boat- kindred spirits on the same vessel.

I can't remember how long I was looking for work but somehow, unemployment compensation sustained us during that time. I had interviewed with every area weekly paper close to home and of course there were no positions available. I never had the courage or credentials to apply to The Boston Globe or The Herald, so I did the next best thing: I applied to a radio station in our area. I got hired!!

WGTR, John Garabedian, Commercials and Getting Fired

Whphen I had exhausted all newspaper possibilities (that I thought I could possibly work for) I went on to the next possibility: radio-advertising sales. Someone I admired greatly was John Garabedian; he owned WGTR, the local station in Natick, MA. John reminded me so much of Howard Stern (who I didn't know about till decades later). John was tall and lanky like Howard, had crazy curly long hair like Howard, and had a wonderful "radio voice," in my opinion better than Howard. John was kind enough to meet with me and ultimately hired me. I was very happy to be back at work and the job was so much closer to home. I hit the road running and soon discovered that selling radio advertising was very different from selling newspaper ad space--so much harder!

While I was struggling to learn the business John had a very interesting idea; he thought I should make radio commercials.

He said there were certain ones that lent themselves to a female voice and since the only other woman at the station had done those commercials in the past, he thought a "new voice" would be appealing to listeners of the station. I can only say that recording those commercials was the most fun I had at that job. Ultimately, John fired me one Friday afternoon. His reason was that I was too timid and not aggressive enough to make it in the business and truth be told, he was right. I had never been fired from a job (up until then) and it was ego shattering. In the end, though, it was a relief; I really didn't like it. Now, I know that along the road of life I am not the only person who has taken a job they were not right for, but getting fired hurts one's ego.

The Eagles

One of the few perks at the radio station was I got to meet a lot of recording reps who called upon John, trying to get their artists more playtime. One of those reps and I became somewhat close and on one of his trips to Boston from Los Angeles he took me to meet The Eagles in their hotel. It was interesting to see a group that was so bright and dynamic on stage be so mild-mannered in person. I was quite surprised. It was one of my few delights during my short-lived career in radio.

Becoming a Cub Scout Leader: Jail, the Auto Plant and the Pinewood Derby

During those early years of working and having my small boys with me, there was always some guilt that nagged at me about not being a stay-at-home mom. Intellectually I knew I was not the only single parent that had to work, but that did not negate my feelings of not being there for my boys. One day, between my radio failure and my next job (whatever it was), there came an opportunity to become a Cub Scout Den Leader and I jumped at the chance to be around my oldest child. My younger son was almost four years younger than his brother and was too young to be a Cub Scout. I have no idea what he was doing when I was "den leading," but it must have been good stuff because he was a great kid.

I really enjoyed myself during those times when I got to be with these eight or ten boys at our meetings. Every now and then I'd get their parents' consent and several other moms would assist me in driving them to an activity outside of Scouts. Two that

I can remember as if it were yesterday are taking them to Jail and going through an auto manufacturing plant.

I had known some volunteer policemen when I was married, and my ex-husband had been one. Fast forward four years after my divorce, and I called one of them and asked if he could possibly arrange a private tour of the jail. He did make it happen and instead of our regular meeting that month, several of us moms took these kids to jail. They were thrilled and unlike their eleven-year-old rowdy behavior that usually came out at our meetings, they were model Scouts that day. It was pretty cool to have the local sheriff take us through the entire jail facility, including their shooting range and the actual lock-ups where they took prisoners after they were charged with a crime of some sort. The boys were excited and when we got to the cells they all went into one. The sheriff shut the door to show them what it was like to be a prisoner. I saw the looks on some of the kids and signaled to the sheriff to let them out immediately. THAT was an exciting day, not only for the boys but for me as well.

Our next adventure, somewhat later in that year, took us to an actual automotive plant that was very close to our home, one town over. Again, with parental consent and another friendly "Scout mom," we drove to the gigantic plant. Now in those days we young women wore short skirts and go-go boots with very high, thin heels. Whatever possessed me to wear those boots is unknown, but I have to tell you, if there was ever a case of wrong decision making, this was it. After we had walked the entire plant, stopping at each part section to hear a quick overview of what the part was, besides the obvious-- steering wheel, engine, wheels, etc.--we ended up at the area where the totally put-together car was going over final inspection. By the time we finished our three hour tour, the boys were exhausted and I could barely walk. I spent most of the night after dinner in a hot tub trying to soothe my aching, swollen feet. The plant director had told us we'd walked a total of four miles traversing each aisle of the plant. I truly believed him; my feet felt like they'd walked at least ten.

The last memorable thing I can remember about my Cub Scout days was the Pinewood Derby, an annual event for all Scouts across the nation. I had no idea that not only did the Cubs have to make their own (with no help from parents, I believe) BUT the den leaders had to make one as well. These little race cars would go down a track and the most accurate aerodynamic one usually won. Well, now that my son and I both had to carve one out of pinewood, we went to the hardware store and asked for help in choosing our supplies. Long story short, my finished car was a disaster and my son did an admirable job but neither of us came close to winning. Years later, as I look down at my left index finger I barely can see the scar anymore where the coping saw slipped as I was sawing and shaping my car.

After a year, both of us were done with Scouting and we both went on to different adventures.

The Mountain, the Ropes
and 103-degree Fever

For many years after I'd moved to Virginia in 1979, I was very involved with the programs associated with EST and Werner Erhard. One of those programs was called "The Six Day Course." The course was held in the mountains of New Paltz, NY and also somewhere in CA. I went to New Paltz to do mine. The reason I'd decided to take this course was to overcome my wimpy fears of not being able to do very physical things. One of the prerequisites of taking this program was that you had to have completed the EST Training and be in excellent physical condition. I had completed the EST Training and had taken many seminars afterward, as well. I can't remember where I had my physical, but I was deemed healthy as a horse. I planned to take the next available SIX DAY and drove up to New Paltz with a girl from my area.

As the name implied, the course took six days to complete and the first several days were quite rigorous. Sitting and "stand up;

sit down" drove some people mad but other than that segment being tedious, I had no trouble with it. I didn't think I was having any issues, until I noticed that I was beginning to get sick: aches and pain all over (like the flu) and a fever. There was a doctor at our location and on a meal break the doctor came to see what the matter was. It was only day 2 of the course and this had come out of nowhere. I really had been completely well when I began the course just one day ago. I thought it most bizarre. I can't remember if the doctor gave me something to take, but I slugged it out to finish the day. For that day and the next I was quite miserable, to the point that I didn't even take a shower (gross as that was). By day four I truly thought I was going to die. My temperature had spiked to 103 degrees and my hands and feet were so weak I could hardly walk.

There was great significance to this day. It was the Ropes Course. Might I also add that it was pouring rain? I now was really sure that I had brought myself here to die. Interestingly, my dear friend Libby from Washington, DC was one of the people who was a volunteer assistant at this six-day event. We were put into groups of four, and Libby was in charge of my group. We all headed out to the mountain where the three activities comprised of traversing between two mountains, rappelling down a mountainside and zip-lining from very high up over to the other side of a lake.

I had told Libby that I didn't think I could make it; my hands were so weak and painful that I knew I couldn't hold on to the ropes. I guess Libby was somewhat nervous about that and told the course leader what condition I was in and he immediately came up to me and said in a very stern voice, "Cut it out." Well, as if I wasn't sick enough, that rebuke really pissed me off and I became determined to be the FIRST in our group to go. So when it was our group's turn at the first event (traversing two mountains), I did say, "Let me go first." They all looked at me skeptically and said okay. Libby put on my helmet and two other assistants buckled me into my harness and I started across the mountain. My tears melded with the torrential rain but I actually was moving myself, hand over hand, quite well when something happened: I stopped in the middle-dead stopped. There I was hanging upside down between two mountains screaming, "I can't do it." All along I could hear my name being chanted by people at the top of each mountain and now they were yelling "you can do it" over and over. All of a sudden something very strange happened; one of my feet hit something solid and people were getting me out of the harness. The doctor grabbed me to break my impending fall and as he held me I was crying so hard I could barely see. He said, "Elaine, look at where you just brought yourself." I whimpered, "No I didn't; someone must have pulled me in," and he said a resounding, "NO-you just did that YOURSELF." No kidding, at that moment the pain left my hands-honest to God, it really did. I stopped crying. I couldn't believe it. Now on the other mountaintop, I cheered my other group members across and when they made it, we headed off to the next obstacle: traversing down the mountain; I think it was 60 or 70 feet straight down. By the way, the rain had stopped, but it was still cloudy and gloomy.

The next event was almost as bad for me. When it was my turn to get harnessed and helmeted up I took one look down and the assistants on the ground looked like ants; that's how far up we were. You had to take the two ropes in both hands, turn around backwards, go to the edge and push off. This one I knew I definitely could not do and I told the very small girl who had strapped me in. Her response was, "Quit your moaning. You've been blubbering all morning and no one wants to hear any more. Turn around, hands on the ropes, feet at the edge, butt out. Now push off." She REALLY pissed me off, so I just did what I was told…and WOW, I didn't fall. In fact I was holding on, yelling like a banshee and moving all over the mountainside instead of going straight down. The next person in my group could not begin their descent until I was safely on the ground, so all the assistants at the bottom kept yelling at me to come down. The truth was that I was having such a glorious time realizing that I was in control and wasn't going to die that I probably took more time than I should have to get to the bottom. I couldn't get the smile off my face!!!

At this time I must tell you about the running. Every morning before our indoors training took place, there was a run through the mountains, very uneven and bumpy and as far as I was concerned, just torture. I've totally blocked it from my memory, but I wouldn't be surprised to learn that I came in LAST every day; I hate running of any sort. I'm sure I'd be eaten if a bear came out of nowhere onto our running course. Anyway, I do remember who came in first every day. Her name eludes me but I remember her to be a flight attendant and in terrific shape.

Boy, could she run fast. I couldn't have cared less about when I finished; I was just trying to preserve my life, and let me say with a 103 degree temperature on day 4 it truly was a matter of life or death for me before we hit the mountain in the pouring cold rain.

It was our last event of the ropes course and I felt so much better--no aches, no pains and no fever as best I could tell. The sun even came out. As we were standing in line to take our group's turn at mounting the very high platform to zip line over the lake, I turned around to see who was crying so hard behind me. It was the young, very fit flight attendant. She told me she was terrified of the zip line. For a minute I couldn't understand why one who flew the skies would be afraid of a little old zip line. I stopped myself from saying something to that effect when my flying days found me fearless and this ropes course was the most terrifying experience of my life.

Being "cured" of all my ills and feeling brave at that moment, I put my arm around her and told her to watch me do it and not to be afraid. I would go last in my group to show her how much fun it was and she could go right after me (first in her group). She stopped crying and thanked me for my kindness. Kindness, phooey! If it hadn't been for my fellow course mates cheering me on, I don't think I could have made it this far. The other three people in my group zipped across with no hesitation and I had to be just as fearless for this girl. After all, I'd been afraid most of the day. After climbing the ladder to this very small ledge I took it all in: the sunny blue sky, the glorious weather (it had warmed up), and the very wide lake I was about to cross on a zip line. I got harnessed in and had my head gear on, and just as the assistant told me to go to the edge, raise my feet and let go, I let it rip: probably one of the most scary, exciting and fun things I had ever done.

That evening, to conclude the ropes course day, we all met to discuss our experiences of the mountain and what the mountains meant to each of us. The first thing the course leader did was call on me to ask if I led seminars for Werner Erhard and Associates. I laughed and said "no." He said he was surprised because he had never seen anyone create such sickness leading up to today. I answered by telling the group how frightened I was of being a wimp and not being capable of doing anything strenuous. I really thought I'd come to this course to prove I could do anything, but ultimately thought I was going to die today-until I didn't. I remember the whole room cheering. Needless to say, I hadn't died and I had conquered the mountain and I was back to perfect health, just the way I had arrived four days earlier.

I took a very long shower that night. I can't remember anything else about day 6. The mountain course was a defining experience in my life and I'm very clear that is why I did the course.

I now think a little more before I say "I can't do that."

THE BEACH- Rehoboth Beach, DL

For over thirty-five years one of the greatest joys of my life was spending time at the beach in Rehoboth Beach, DL. I'd say that in the beginning it was a group of thirty-somethings: maybe eight to ten of us girls who poured into several cars and would head off to the beach on a Friday afternoon after work. There was this "reasonable" motel about half a block from the boardwalk. If we squeezed four girls to a room, we could often be able to stay for the weekend. We shared Fourth of Julys at the beach as well as Memorial Day weekends and alas, the final weekend of summer when The Royal Treat (our favorite breakfast spot) closed. Although there usually were many more weeks that remained warm, going to the beach without starting our day at the Royal Treat wasn't quite the same experience.

There were years when I was married again that my grown children would join us at the beach for a weekend. When my oldest son got married, he and his wife would come, as well as her mother. There are great memories of those times. But probably the best times, as weird as it may sound, are the last fifteen years, before I moved to NC, when I went to Rehoboth by myself. Each trip was like a small, miraculous Zen adventure.

At the age of about fifty-seven, none of my friends would hit the road at 4:45 am to make the two and a half hour trek to the beach; they all thought I was a little crazy to do this at my age, but for me, it was very special "down time" after a hectic week of work. My sweet partner Rick had no issue with my choice: the beach was never a high priority for him and he knew how important it was for me.

In the summer months there was at least one weekend day that was beach-worthy and that was the day I'd go. The day began with leaving our home in Bethesda, MD no later than 4:45 am and driving to our local 7-11 to grab a very large cup of high test coffee; that would keep me up and alert for the ride. The game was ALWAYS to get over the Bay Bridge by 6:00 am-that was the magic time that meant I would beat the beach traffic and have smooth sailing all the way. If I didn't have a full tank of gas I'd stop and fill up after the bridge. The gas was always cheaper.

The next hour and a half was beautiful, very rural. Corn and vegetable fields were all around and it was the beginning of a very tranquil day. The small towns I passed always reminded me of times gone by. To arrive at Rehoboth Avenue around 7:30 am allowed for a great parking space for the day, but also gave some time to become what would begin a very long line to the Royal Treat when it opened at 8:00 am. Over the years I came to know some of the "first seating" regulars. Besides getting to the beach early, having breakfast at the Royal Treat was such an awesome experience--so much so that I wrote an article about it in the October 2012 issue of Delaware *Beach Life* magazine. After the same breakfast of Fat French toast, sausage and coffee, it was off to the beach. For thirty-five years I ALWAYS ate the same breakfast-no kidding, but the beach was a different thing.

In the early days, the girls and I would sit mid beach, just far away from families with screaming little kids, but not too far from the water for those of us that liked to dunk or swim. There was one weekend that my kids were visiting when the water came up to the boardwalk during a very high tide.

Over time, the city of Rehoboth Beach widened the beach and added beach grass and a high dune. That feature really expanded the sand part of the beach and gave me the option, when I was by myself, to sit at the very back of the beach, where very few people sat. With a beach umbrella and my chair, I could sleep and read for hours and be very close to the boardwalk when it was time for lunch or a cool drink. It was very soothing; I could still hear the waves and see the ocean.

As years went by and I was no longer working, I was so fortunate to find a wonderful guest house half a block from the beach and one block over from the Royal Treat. What made it such fun was the fact that I could park in the yard (no parking meter-yeah), as well as sharing the bathroom with other guests and an outside shower. A clothesline was in the back yard and right next to the shower. I loved it!!! I could check the weather for any time in the week, call the owners and if they had a room, I'd pack up and go for a couple of days. I think Rick came with me several times and enjoyed himself.

We have friends who have a year round house in Rehoboth Beach and at least one weekend per season we were invited to visit. That weekend, we'd always hit the outlets to shop.

When Rick and I decided we were relocating to NC, I made the summer before our move a very special event. Knowing that this would be my last season at "my beach" (also known as America's vacation spot), I truly savored every day I had there.

In the end, having my last breakfast at the Royal Treat was akin to eating the best meal I'd ever had. It truly was like saying goodbye to a very close friend, and as I headed for home I thought of all the wonderful years I had shared with dear friends and family and the tranquility I'd so appreciated, as well as the difference being there had made to me.

DC Jail and Coaching

Over the years, after the Six Day Course, I continued to participate in the EST seminars. In fact, for the last thirty-seven years I had been in at least two seminars a year and completed many programs. This stopped when I moved to NC in 2011 because the nearest seminars were in Raleigh, several hours from where I now live.

In the early to mid-80s I made lasting friendships with other people who had also done the training and were in seminars with me. One of the most flamboyant and charming guys was named Charles. Charles was a fabulous hairdresser and had two salons in DC. Charles and I got to know each other quite well over time and on one occasion he told me he was friends with the Mayor. Apparently there were no programs in the DC jail for women offenders. Men had lots of opportunities to learn a trade but there was no money available for such programs for the women. The Mayor went to Charles and asked him if he could create a program that might afford these women the possibility of getting a job when they got out of jail. Charles, being the generous man that he was, naturally agreed. Charles wasn't quite sure how to put this together so he asked some of his friends to join him in this endeavor. I was one of those people.

Everyone else was very qualified, as I recall, to impart some good coaching to these women; as far as I was concerned I wasn't sure what I could contribute. Charles said he had heard me share in many of our seminars over the years and he was convinced that even if I went in and just shared some of my life experiences, these women would ultimately come away with something useful. I said okay and was in 100%.

There was no training for us, and the afternoon of my first visit to the jail, I was totally on my own. The DC jail is quite large and a far cry from the local small jail I took my Scouts to years before. There are many very dangerous criminals housed in the DC jail and I was a little apprehensive, not knowing what kind of women I would come in contact with. After signing in at the "guest station" and showing my ID and explaining why I was there, I was escorted to a room. I must tell you that everything was painted that obnoxious industrial green color and was just yucky. I often wondered if someone had decided it was a soothing color for the inmates, but who cared what I thought?

There were about ten or twelve women already in the room when I arrived. They all had very hard looks on their faces and

I knew I had my work cut out for me. After introducing myself, I asked them if they wouldn't mind telling me their names and what they were incarcerated for in, other words, what had they done to get themselves into this mess? They laughed (a good sign, I thought) and went around the room and told me their stories. Most were in for theft or drugs. To my amazement, one young woman had been arrested three times for shoplifting at Saks Fifth Avenue. She said that was her favorite store. Everyone laughed. I told them that the definition of insanity was doing the same thing over and over and expecting a different result. No one laughed but they got some food for thought. Thank goodness, no murderers! What a relief. I was surprised at how young most of them were. With the exception of two girls, the room was filled with black women and that's probably due to the disproportionate amount of blacks to whites who resided in the District of Columbia.

I began by telling them that I really didn't know what to speak to them about and that got a laugh!! "Would you mind if we all wear name tags?" I asked. I knew that they all knew each other, but I had a rotten memory and didn't want to stress over forgetting their names. After they all agreed, I went into my pocketbook and pulled out some nametags: I'd come prepared, hoping they'd agree. During the two sessions I met with these women, we discussed: 1.When you get out of jail, don't come back. 2. Start thinking of yourself as worthy; you can't remove the things that got you locked up in the first place but you can take responsibility for what you've done: OWN IT and begin to create a new life, if you choose. 3. Groom yourself well.

First impressions count. If a prospective employer sees that you take care of yourself, he might see that you can take care of his business. 4. If you want a job as a cook, don't apply for a job as a cleaning lady.

When we were all finished with our coaching sessions, a graduation was planned. I don't know if Charles supplied the caps and gowns, but the women smiled like Cheshire cats when all the coaches showed up to cheer them on as an official of the jail gave out their diplomas and thanked us for what we had contributed.

A final note: several months after we'd finished at the jail I heard that one of the women that we coached had been released from jail and had been hired as a cook at a country club in Northern Virginia. It's something she had always wanted to do but drug use had gotten in her way. Apparently she got clean while in jail and finally had the courage to apply for the job. I hope I had a little something to do with her newfound confidence in herself. The whole experience was very gratifying. I really got a true sense of myself and that I was qualified to coach people.

Property Management Association

Aside from my scooping days at the Newport Creamery and my short-lived life as an airline stewardess, the work opportunity that was the most rewarding began in the late 80's through the mid- 1990's. I had been in sales for many years when this job opening occurred. More about the job later. I want to talk about PMA.

It was 1989 and the Berlin Wall had just come down. Lucille Ball had just died. There was a worldwide ban on Ivory. Pan Am Airlines had filed for Chapter 11 bankruptcy and Pete Rose had been banned from baseball for illegal gambling.

I was a one-woman show in this new job that I had. I lived in Baltimore at the time but commuted to Washington, DC for work. I knew no one in business in the DC area and found the Property Management Association the perfect organization to join. My employer (out of Memphis, TN) agreed and paid for my membership. There were probably more vendors than property managers in the association. I didn't care; I just needed a group where I could meet potential customers. Over the years I made some lasting friendships that are very important to me to this day. Thank goodness there was someone who took me around to meet people at the very first meeting I attended. I liked these people very much. There weren't any other vendors at that time that represented my product in PMA, so in that regard no other vendor was my competition and therefore, no one hesitated to become my friend. Funny as it may seem, I gravitated to more women than men, even though I got more business from men than women-go figure.

One of the first things I did, after I knew the ropes was to join the Associates Council that was comprised of vendors of PMA. Wow, they were such an active and diverse group, and very dedicated. The associates met once a month at 7:30 am, which required me to be on the road by 6:30 am. I did this for years, with joy. When it came time to choose a leader for the year, and I guess because I was nobody's competitor, I was nominated. I'd like to think it was because of some skills that I possessed but let's be real, no one saw me as a threat to their business. It truly was a glorious year. I had the most wonderful vice-chairperson as my right-hand gal and she helped me so much as we took on many programs for the association.

I know I accomplished one very big feat that year: I had noticed early on that when we all went to the PMA monthly meetings, the property managers wore one color name tag and the associates wore another color. What that did in my opinion was actually keep the two groups apart, because no property manager wanted to be put in a tight spot with a vendor. I really had not met anyone who I thought would do such a thing so I brought my concern to the board of directors (which I was a part of that year, 1995). I guess my unease with the nametags resonated with most board members and when a vote to have the nametags all one color came to be, it passed and to the best of my knowledge it still remains in effect (21 years later). I guess this was such a radical change for the association that with a little prodding from my vice-chair, I was voted Associate of the Year.

Energy Conservation Stories and the "One Year I'll keep my Word" Event

The year was also 1989. I was married and living in a suburb of Baltimore, when an interesting job opportunity came my way. A friend of a friend knew I'd been in sales for a long time and was very good at whatever I was selling. My last job had been selling long-distance phone service where people had to pay $10.00 to join. I suppose this guy thought that if I could be a re-seller of AT&T and charge people for it, I could sell anything.

My meeting with the owners of this company (honestly, I can't remember the Baltimore company's name) was very intriguing and the product I was to sell resonated with me at the highest level. Boy, was I wrong. After a while all my altruistic thinking went out the door and I found the way to sell. I was interviewed and offered the job!

Another woman and I were hired that day. We were representing a silver reflector for commercial 2'x4' light fixtures that allowed you to remove two of the light tubes and one ballast, and center the remaining two lamps in front of the optical reflectors. This would allow for half the energy use per fixture without diminishing the light quality, which would equal half the money spent to run a fixture. Our company was the mid-Atlantic rep for a firm out of Memphis, TN called Energy Design Corporation. It sounded very challenging - and who wouldn't want to save energy, right?

The first thing after being hired, I asked to be allowed to set up an office in Washington, DC. This was met with great resistance, as you can imagine. First of all there was no money for an office in DC, but as I explained that my entire sphere of influence was in the metropolitan DC area they started to relent. I also told them I didn't think I could "get in a door" in Baltimore because I had not grown up in Baltimore, and unlike DC, where everyone is from somewhere else, Baltimore is a very tight-knit small city. Thus when someone would ask, "Where'd you go to high school, hon?" I would not have a satisfactory answer. The owners said they'd think about it and I bravely said I couldn't accept the job if I couldn't work from Washington. "And besides," I said, "that way the other girl and I would have defined areas to work and would not fight over leads or buildings." They thought about this for several minutes and then asked me if I thought I could find a space for a certain sum per month (I can't remember how much). I said I'd give it a try and thus began my most fun career that I thought would last forever. Monday morning I got in the car and drove to DC, riding up and down streets to see if there were any signs on buildings saying "Office space for rent." In one day I hit the jackpot.

For anyone who knows DC, 15th street, two blocks from Pennsylvania Avenue, across from the Treasury Department and close to the White House, is a prime location in to have an office. I couldn't believe the sign read EXECUTIVE OFFICE SUITES FOR RENT. It was a gorgeous old building, and after I found a parking space (not so easy), I went to visit with the manager and find out what an "executive suite" entailed. First off, the rent was ridiculously low by DC standards, especially in such a perfect location. The manager explained that the building was due for a major renovation or tear down and they wanted to keep tenants for as long as they could, therefore they were offering below-market rates. The office that was to be mine was unbelievable. Twenty-foot ceiling, old-fashioned radiator (the room was toasty warm: I can't stand being cold) and even a chandelier for a light fixture. I imagined that the entire building had once been a very large mansion. What made it an "executive suite" was that there were a series of offices around a large open area that provided typing services, a message center, fax and copy machines, and a lunchroom. A desk, chairs, file cabinet, curtains on the large windows, phone and coat tree were provided in the rent (phone use was charged extra). If I used any of the other services, I would be charged. I called my bosses to get approval and they immediately said, "Take it." I was so under budget that I asked if I could put the car in a garage close to my building and even with that monthly charge it kept me in line and they said, "Okay." What a first day of work that had been! Now we could print up business cards - I had a home.

The next day I set up my office in less than an hour; after all, I had very little to put in it. The men from Energy Design said they'd be up the following week to meet with the gang in Baltimore and me in DC. Since I didn't have a clue how to sell this optical reflector made by 3M, I spent the rest of the week scouting the area on foot. There were many office buildings in my immediate location so day in and day out, I would explore building by building on foot to get a sense of which ones might be potential customers. The men from Memphis were bringing us small reflectors and lamps for demonstration the following week. Trust me, the boys in Baltimore knew as much as we sales reps did; nothing-so we all looked forward to being trained, so to speak. Let me quickly tell you about ALL buildings in downtown DC. No building can be higher than 13 stories, allowing full view of the Capital, the Washington Monument and the Lincoln Memorial. Across the Potomac River, buildings soared because they were in Northern Virginia and didn't have the same height restrictions as DC.

The second week of work, the Memphis men came, meeting first with the Baltimore folks and later in the week with me. I think they spent more time with me because they'd actually retrofitted a building in Washington and I would have the benefit of being able to show a prospective client an "already done" building. They came with a handful of Energy Design Corporation glossy folders containing materials on the company, 3M and maybe a client list; I'm not sure. I do remember everything being of very good quality and very professional. I would be pleased to leave one with anyone who showed a modicum of interest. Next came the baby reflectors and lamps, small enough to carry around and demonstrate. They showed me how to explain the process and how it could benefit the potential client. They took me to visit people they had already met with when THEY used to come to DC to sell. Needless to say, they were very pleased to have someone here who was local and knew her way around. Lacking any real confidence that I knew how to actually sell the product, I made them commit to come to DC any time I needed them. Of course they said "yes". After they left I finally got myself prepared to call on a building manager and see how I'd do talking about my product.

Prior to my first outing I'd gone to an Army-Navy store and found a green mechanic's bag that was the perfect size for carrying my baby light fixture and reflector. I've got to tell you, I was quite bold and on my first day out, after having scouted the area, I called on The National Press Building. I chose that building because it was only two blocks from my office, was an entire block long in size, and as far as I could see, the lights never went out. The building was up and running 24/7. A perfect candidate for my product.

Without an appointment I wasn't sure I'd even get past a gate keeper to see the property manager, but given my office was only two blocks away and I'd walked, I figured why not go for it. I learned very quickly on my visit that making an appointment was the way to go with this property manager (from this point on they shall all be known as PMs) and so I made one for the following day. Having this knowledge served me well. For the rest of the day, I walked from building to building attempting to get appointments with PMs. I'd say maybe one out of five would let me even make a date to see them.

A decision was made that first real day out in the field to make a series of appointments (as many as I could) and then concentrate all my energy on whichever one "blinked first." I really had my heart set on the National Press Building (NPB) because the building was huge and I knew I could make them so energy efficient. I was in for a very rude awakening! I put a quick call into Memphis. Because the folks in Baltimore knew very little about the process of selling this concept of reflectors, the folks at EDC became my only source for knowledge. After all, they had done it before. Gary and John were wonderful and were always a great support as well as excellent teachers. I told them that I had an appointment and knew how to make my presentation, but after having done that, what was next? Now this was the "un-fun" part of the job. In truth, this was the ONLY part of the job that was labor-intensive and required a great deal of time and stamina from me. If I got past the presentation, I was then to ask if I could audit the building. If YES (and why wouldn't they say okay?) I was to count every

2'x4' light fixture in the building. A side note: so far all of this, including an analysis of my findings, was free to the building. No money ever was seen until someone committed to the job being done. This could take months, as I soon discovered. This was truly "on the job training."

My appointment the next day went very well. This was my first true experience of demonstrating the baby reflector, and it went off without a hitch. At the end I asked if I could audit the building and with a modest amount of skepticism the PM said yes. I was thrilled. There was one logistical problem, though. Every tenant in the building had to be notified that I would be walking through their office space, counting light fixtures. The management informed the tenants and there was no pushback on their part, so with a scheduled date of the middle of the following week, I got prepared.

Let's go back a little: one of the first things I had to do was become partners with the local utility. I was definitely not their friend; after all, I wanted to cut the building's lighting energy consumption by one half. Half the lighting electrical use meant a great deal of money coming off the building's bill; good for the building but bad for Potomac Electric Power Company (PEPCO: the DC and part of MD utility company). All I can say is how happy I was when I realized I didn't really need them in those early days. Our partnership really didn't begin until 1990. So back to the National Press Building.

In order to do this properly I should have had a "counter" to keep track of the fixtures in each office, as well as any bathrooms and some hallways that were common areas to the building. Not knowing that at the time, it truly was a miracle that I got the count right! Next came my clothing. I couldn't wear a dress or heels to walk a building. I needed to wear some kind of pants and very comfortable shoes; walking a building means you're on your feet for hours. The count went much better than I thought and when I was finished, I asked the PM if I could see the building utility bill so I could gather the information I needed to give them a written proposal and the results from the walk-through audit. Little did they know the proposal was being generated from the Memphis office. I had no computer skills and since this was my first proposal, I couldn't take the chance that I'd screw up. Mary, the wonderful secretary from EDC in Memphis, typed it up for me, with Gary's precise information, and faxed it up to me, with a copy going to our Baltimore office.

I couldn't believe it when I saw the numbers: there were thousands of light fixtures in the building and factoring in the price the NPB paid for lighting electricity divided by two gave a pretty accurate picture of how much energy they would be saving and how much money they would save on a yearly basis. The money alone was over a quarter of a million dollars. Naturally, when I delivered the final proposal to the PM, I expected a very big smile on his face, but quite to the contrary, he thanked me for the proposal and without a smile or even looking at all that had been prepared for him, he said, "Thanks and I'll get to it when I have the time." That reaction was so unexpected that I vowed to myself to rein in my expectations and never count on anything being a done deal until the ink is on the paper and the paper is in my hand. I left that day somewhat dejected.

Fast forward about a month. Every five days I walked to the National Press Building to see the PM. If I was lucky, he'd come out of his office and tell me he really hadn't had the time to look things over. With my frustration "stuffed," I'd ask him to PLEASE take some time to see all the savings and let me answer any questions he might have. I said I'd stop by again the following week. On my fourth visit, as I was waiting to see him, an older gentleman came out of another office and asked who I was there to see. When I told him why I was waiting he said, "Are you the woman who has been disrupting this office, and for that matter, the whole building?" I said yes and shared with him my frustration at not being able to find anyone who represented the building owner and had his interest at heart. After all, saving the building a quarter of a million dollars was nothing to ignore and I had hoped the PM would take my proposal seriously and pass it on to the building owner.

This man said that he represented the owner and he took the owner's money very seriously (I thought I would faint-this was just too awesome). He went into the PM's office, retrieved the proposal and invited me into his office to go over my proposal and help him understand how I came up with my numbers. It truly was not rocket science and as I went over everything, he understood it immediately. He asked for references and when I offered to take him to a building we had already retrofitted, he said that it wasn't necessary, since he knew that owner of that building as well. He said he'd get back to me, and in three days I had my first contract AND the ink had dried.

Now this contract presented one logistical challenge: I had included labor in my pricing but had no one to install the product. I had gone to an electrical contractor who said that they had no interest in this kind of work. The people who had done the work for the first building the Memphis guys had retrofitted were no longer in business. My bosses in Baltimore could find no one to do the work so I couldn't believe that I was left holding the bag, so to speak. I told my husband what the situation was and he said he could do the work. I was flabbergasted. He was between jobs and said he could enroll some men who could use the money. The installation process was done at night. I asked him if he could live with the labor pricing (The Memphis guys had priced everything) and he said yes.

Well, time went by, the reflectors got built, the crew was formed and did the work well, the client was very happy and I was over the moon. The job from my first visit to completion took about four months (I'm guessing) and in the meantime I had the possibility of another project in process. As time went by and I had been so successful with the NPB, I got a call out of the blue from the president of Energy Design. He asked me if I was interested in going to work for them directly. Wow-the first employee not from Memphis. I would be a Vice-President, Mid-Atlantic Region. They also would put me on salary as well as commission and it would be more than I was currently making. I would have to close the DC office and they would pay for a new one, more centrally located, so I could handle MD as well as VA and the District. What was not to like? They assured me that they would handle the upset with the Baltimore people when they told them I would be working for Memphis directly. Well, there was an explosion in Baltimore and they came to DC and closed up my office and took everything that they felt belonged to them. It was not pleasant.

My new adventure required me to find a new office in the MD suburbs. I looked for another Executive Suite, as I really had loved the one in DC. I found one in a fabulous office in a much more modern space and within one week I was up and running. I still concentrated heavily on DC because the energy costs were more than in MD and I found out very quickly that VA had the lowest utility rates around and had no interest in my product. After hearing that I was peddling "snake oil" (said to me by the director of engineering at a large DC college), I decided to stop taking my little reflector on appointments and chose a different path. I hired a new photographer I had recently met at an association event and asked him if he'd take pictures of the buildings that I'd transformed. He said "yes" and his rates were OK with Memphis, so for the next several years, as I completed one building after another, he would meet me on a Sunday afternoon and he would photograph the outside of the building in glorious color and I would compile a fact sheet:

before and after costs, savings, etc. As my small portfolio grew, the selling cycle got much shorter. Often, all I'd have to do was show my building pages and I'd get the okay to audit a building and give a proposal.

In 1989 I was driving around DC in the middle of the night, identifying buildings that had their lights on. One such building was called Metropolitan Square and it was a beauty. Like the NPB it was huge and filled with many prestigious law firms. Lawyers in Washington often work very long hours and at 2:00am half the building had lights burning bright. This was my next prospect. Two days later I drove to the building, found the management office, walked in (minus an appointment) and asked to see the PM. As luck would have it she was free for a few minutes and the secretary walked me to her office. Sandy was a charming woman and told me she could not make an appointment with me for a year. She said she was new to the building and had a crisis to deal with. There was a leak coming from somewhere on the roof and water was coming down the walls of one of her tenants, possibly threatening their computers. She said, "Come back in a year." I asked if she meant it and she said yes. I took out my calendar and made a note to call for an appointment a year from that day. I told her I would not bother her again and would keep my word by setting something up in one year. I asked her to put something on her calendar to set up an appointment with me in one year as well.

For one year I didn't go near her building and on that day in 1990 I called and made an appointment. Long story short, after going through the entire process and a bidding war with her "light bulb salesman," I got the job. This was huge. She said she awarded me the project because I was the only salesperson she had ever met who kept their word. She said she knew I would get the job done with very little disturbance of her tenants. Someone with that much integrity would not allow for any mishaps.

In the meantime, Potomac Electric Power Company (PEPCO), the local utility company, created the Trade Ally Program (we vendors were the allies) to rebate buildings that made energy saving modifications to their building(s). This now was an extra incentive for the owners to consider, as this rebate program gave money back to the buildings from the utility, making their return on investment much sooner than before the inception of this program. How quickly I, and all my competitors (they came out of the woodwork), became friends of the utility. Now, saving energy was very attractive. The more energy saved, the better for the utility. The electric grid that ran through the Mid-Atlantic was coming close to capacity and more electricity had to be freed up. My project and anything else that saved electricity was king.

I had many possibilities in the pipeline and for once the utility was my best friend in business. I filled out their required paperwork properly, got all their requirements in order and complied with all they asked for. I was a very good partner in this new program. I must say that during this time that I was "on fire;" rumor had it that one of my competitors was spreading rumors about how and why I got so many projects. It was quite nasty--after all, I had been the first woman "on the streets" selling energy efficiency. It was also sexist. I had no time for this type of garbage, but I did take time out of my day to write him a "thank you note" thanking him for thinking I had that much energy to retrofit all the buildings I had and still had time to engage in so-called "extracurricular activities with every building engineer in DC and MD," if you get my drift. WINNING was the best revenge.

Awards-Awards-Awards

The year was 1991 and I could hardly keep up with the workload-it was glorious. I knew I could stay in this business forever. During the almost two years I had worked for EDC I had gone to Memphis several times for company meetings. By now they had hired a man in New Jersey and one in Texas to be VPs of their respective regions. At one of these meetings, the owner announced he had decided to change the spelling of our company to **Energy Dezign Corporation**. There was no doubt that my area was HOT due to this rebate program and I think I had a much easier time selling our product, but truthfully, this name change just added an unnecessary layer to a conversation. When a prospect asked why the company had changed the spelling of DESIGN to DEZIGN, all I could say was the owner wanted to do it. Gary (the president of EDC) was great, but he was a little quirky.

My portfolio had some beautiful buildings to show and thousands of dollars of rebates for each building. Near the end of 1990 I had sold the entire office park where I had my office. This was comprised of five buildings and when the months-long project was complete, a representative from PEPCO came out with me to meet with the management and presented them with one of those huge checks for almost $300,000.00. This gesture, along with their real check, was the frosting on the cake. My job was definitely secure.

Unbeknownst to any of us, PEPCO called a huge meeting of their allies to acknowledge the vendors for their partnership in making the Power Savers Program a huge success. The ballroom of the Marriott was jam-packed with very large company contingencies, and as I was the only one from my company, I sat in the back of the room with other small companies. First they explained that they had been keeping track of all the energy saved by each vendor and were here to reward their efforts from the inception. I thought, *"How nice"*. This was a surprise to everyone in the room.

About halfway through the program they announced the award for something (it didn't say for what on the award) and said, "Would a representative from Energy Dezign Corporation come forward?" The whole room, including me, let out a gasp. Yikes, it was like getting an Academy Award and because no one thinks you're a possible winner, you are seated at the back of the huge venue. I worked my way up to the front podium and accepted this small award with gratitude. I had just returned to my table and was passing around this very nice piece of Lucite with my company's name engraved on it when the PEPCO person said, "This next award goes to the company that made the Largest Single KW (kilowatt) Reduction in 1991. Would a representative from Energy Dezign Corporation come forward?" I almost fainted and this time as I managed to get to the podium the whispers could be heard by all. As I thanked them and took my LARGE and heavy award, the PEPCO person said to me softly, "Stay up here, please." The final award was for the Largest Cumulative KW Reduction: 1991. "Would a representative from Energy Dezign Corporation come forward?" He turned to me and smiled. "Oh, you're here" and the room exploded with applause and laughter. I could hardly stand and carry these two heavy Lucite things. As I headed out of the room (I had won the two highest honors for the year) a few kind people (mostly from PEPCO) congratulated me. I took the rest of the day off.

They skipped 1992 but in 1993, the awards got smaller and lighter and I was given an award for being in the "GOLD CLUB," whatever that meant. I was proud to have my four awards. All my hard work had paid off. Coinciding with the PEPCO program, a new organization called the Association of Professional Energy Managers (APEM) was formed by members of PEPCO, the Architect of the Capitol and the energy directors of a huge real estate management company. I was eligible to be a member, even though I was certainly not a part of the energy management community, but because of how significantly I had contributed to the PEPCO program.

During my Energy Dezign years I was not only involved with PMA but became the President of APEM in 1995. That year, after many retrofits, the association invited me to speak at their conference in Long Beach, CA on the docked Queen Mary ocean liner. They paid my expenses, and I was so honored to represent my company and my Chapter. Backtracking to the inception of the PEPCO rebate program, I was asked to sit on a panel at the Environmental Protection Agency to advise on lighting retrofits with optical reflectors. I was invited to write several articles for the EPA newsletter on my projects, which included actual statistics and pictures of the buildings. I got permission from the company managers to share their savings. This newsletter went to every EPA employee in the country. For one person, I was given so many great opportunities and was well respected in my field.

I was truly enjoying my professional years when two unimaginable events occurred: PEPCO stopped the rebate program in 1996 AND Energy Dezign Corporation closed its doors for good. I absolutely saw neither of these events coming. It was a total shock. My career in reflector sales ended very abruptly. I closed down my MD office and headed for home, once again UNEMPLOYED. Thank goodness, it was short-lived.

Baltimore Gas and Electric

As it turned out, one of my former competitors, a very successful young guy who had worked for Sylvania and sold light bulbs, had gone to work for BG&E, the Baltimore utility company. He called me and asked me if I'd like to come to work for him in Baltimore. There was no hesitation on my part. For the past eight years I had been commuting to Washington, DC and MD (close to DC). The thought of starting most days from a Baltimore office (six miles from my home) was so appealing that I couldn't wait to begin. The irony was, I ended up calling on all my former clients. That year PEPCO and BG&E were attempting to merge. While that was going on, our group of salespeople were actively seeking more energy efficient products, even though I can't remember if BG&E had any kind of incentive program.

I happily returned to DC and had a modicum of success selling many more products than I had available at EDC. I also joined another association that BG&E thought would be useful to my efforts. The Apartment and Office Building Association (AOBA) was comprised of management company executives, property managers and vendors. It was bold to enter this arena, as I now worked for BG&E, but the PEPCO representative explained to the utility committee (the one I joined) that a merge negotiation was going on between the two utilities and I was welcomed. I was known to many of these people, so I never felt awkward being there in Washington again. I had a very fruitful year at BG&E, until the merger fell through and our group was disbanded. I was unemployed once again!!!

Water Conservation and Men in Black

By this time in life I'd had more success than failure. For the next year or two, until the year 2000, I made a lifetime of bad choices. It began with my thinking I could sell ANYTHING, and I interviewed with a company that sold water conservation in TOILETS. What was I thinking???? As in most cases, I was hired. To say I hadn't a clue how to sell anything involving toilets is an understatement. After a while I was truly miserable and felt guilty about even taking a paycheck. We were going to attend a trade show and we needed a backdrop for our booth. It was the year of the Men in Black movie and I thought it would be fun to have a backdrop made that spoofed the movie.

One beautiful day, the owner of the company, his son and I put on our black suits and dark sunglasses and proceeded to the back field of their home office building. It truly was beautiful. What made this so compelling were the three toilets that were put in front of us. We posed with our arms folded and our legs apart, behind the toilets as a professional photographer snapped away. The backdrop turned out great and everyone knew what we were pretending to be but as fate would have it, I was a total failure at this job. I stuck it out until the middle of 1999 and graciously left the company. I've often thought, in retrospect, it's good to fail from time to time, and I've always said, "That which doesn't kill us makes us stronger." I started looking for another job; AGAIN.

The Gaithersburg, MD Police Department

The year was 1998 and I was fifty-eight years old. Titanic won the "best picture" award at the Academy Awards. Monica Lewinsky and President Clinton denied having relations with each other. Washington National Airport had been renamed after Ronald Reagan. Elton John had been knighted by Queen Elizabeth and I'd recently gone through a divorce and had moved to Gaithersburg, MD, a small town twenty miles north of Washington, DC. I found a reasonably priced one-bedroom apartment and only brought the things I really treasured from my Baltimore home. One day I was networking with someone who might have influence in helping me get a job. Out of the blue this woman said, "Gaithersburg--are you sure you're safe where you live?" SAFE! It never occurred to me that my environment wasn't safe. Heck, here I was a middle-aged woman, now living alone. I definitely had to take action.

I called the Gaithersburg Police Department and asked if they had any programs for civilians. They said they had two programs and suggested I come to the Community Policing Program. My days were spent looking for work and my nights were spent with girlfriends or taking courses. I was happy being alone; it was a time to heal. It was very rewarding to take this six-week program with the local police. We met once a week and did various police duties such as using a radar gun in traffic, visiting the 911 emergency headquarters, doing a ride-along one night for four hours with a patrolman (there were two incidents that night; I had to stay in the patrol car), and one night watching a police dog perform its duties. At the end of the course I really felt very respectful of what my police department dealt with, BUT it didn't give me the sense of having my own personal safety. That would be handled in their next opportunity.

R.A.D Training

The next opportunity was one designed specifically for women. The program was called The R.A.D Systems of Self-Defense. R.A.D. stood for Rape, Aggression, and Defense. This was just what I was looking for--a basic physical defense course for women. The story goes that that Lawrence Nadeau, while in college, created this program for his mother. I liked that. In a nutshell, about twelve or fifteen women participated in this multi-week course to learn the following: Basic principles of defense, the hand as a weapon, vulnerable locations, offensive and defensive posture, risk reduction, the decision to resist--things like that. When the course was complete I felt very confident that I would never appear vulnerable and I was empowered, I actually used a non-violent action once when the only two people on a street were a young man and me. We were on opposite sides of the street, walking in the same direction. He started to cross the street and was walking toward me when I stopped, took the stance and screamed "STOP" in a very loud voice. He was so startled that he turned away and went back across the street and headed in the opposite direction. I watched as he walked away. My heart was definitely racing but I did avert "who knows what." I took the course again when I was seventy-two. I recommend the R.A.D. program for every woman, no matter her age.

A Romance Odyssey

The year was 2000. The world ushered in the new millennium, Sydney, Australia hosted the Olympics and I was at the point of finally beginning a very good new job. It was May, Memorial Day weekend, Friday. I had volunteered to be part of the AOBA contingency at MD Special Olympics. It was a beautiful sunny day and I stayed all day to support the athletes in any way requested. I was very excited. I was to begin my job the following week; I was going to the beach on Saturday-all was right with the world. When I returned home late Friday, there was a voice message on my phone. This lovely man who I'd known professionally for about ten years had called to ask me to dinner on Sunday night. He apologized for it being such short notice and asked if I was free, to please call him. His name was Rick.

I was quite nervous. In the two years since my divorce I'd only had one dating experience and it was a disaster. I had been perfectly happy being single again and really had no interest in men, but this man was a perfect gentleman, as I recalled, and though you never know how a person is outside of their business persona, I called him back and accepted, insisting I drive myself to the restaurant (in case the date turned out to be a total bust). The beach was glorious on Saturday and Sunday was beautiful as well. As I dressed that night for my date the apprehension grew stronger.

When I arrived at the charming Italian restaurant he'd chosen, I discovered I had arrived first and did the only thing I thought to do: I went directly to the bar. I ordered a glass of wine and as time went by and he wasn't there yet I really started to get nervous. The second glass of wine was almost done when I saw him enter the restaurant. He saw me at the bar and was smiling as he walked toward me. He kissed me on the cheek, as I recall, paid for my drinks and escorted me to our table. The rest is somewhat of a blurred memory. I was practically drunk (I can't have two glasses of wine) and could hardly eat my pasta because I was so charmed by this gorgeous man. I felt like a teenager having her first date. I had three cups of coffee when dinner was complete and assured him I was safe enough to drive myself home. He gently kissed me on the cheek again and sent me on my way.

I knew he would never call again. How embarrassing to get tipsy on your first date. But I had nothing to fear: he called again and this time invited me to his home for dinner. As it turned out we were very compatible; he was an excellent cook and I am an expert "cleaner upper." We dated very quietly for six months before we went public and sixteen years later we're still together and very much in love. As a couple we've shared many wonderful and sad events and each one brought us closer. We will be each other's soul mate until we die, and who knows, maybe even after.

Mentoring and Elizabeth Arden

had moved in with my sweetheart in the winter of 2001 and life together was wonderful. My job was great and I was very happy. My new life was more than I could have asked for. The time had come for me to "give back" in some way. I can't remember how I found out about the opportunity to mentor young women who were transitioning from jail to the outside world again. Well, I certainly had some experience in this arena, so I applied to be a mentor. This was a very structured program, quite different from the DC jail experience. Each woman was assigned one young woman to mentor and each week we all met at a church with our mentees and had a specific program to follow. Every week was different. One week we'd have a speaker on subjects such as dressing for success, resume writing, how to conduct yourself during and after a job interview, role-playing, etc. I think we mentors got just as much out of this program as the girls did. The girls were really working hard and the director and I wanted to do something special for them. Did I mention that this was a volunteer program and all of these young women had freely chosen to participate? That commitment made working with them very easy and they were so eager to turn themselves around and get some great coaching before they set out into their new world.

Our meeting place was right next to a very upscale strip mall comprised of an art gallery, children's clothing store, women's' fashions, several restaurants, a gift store and an Elizabeth Arden Salon. One early evening before the girls arrived via bus from their halfway housing, I walked into Elizabeth Arden and asked to see the manager. He graciously listened as I asked if he'd be willing to work with us in providing a very special treat for our mentees. My vision was that he'd close the salon early on the night we held our course. He would allow each girl to choose two services such as a manicure-pedicure, facial-haircut, etc. and he would do this for free.

The program would supply tips to his workers who provided these services but everything else was on Elizabeth Arden. Imagine my surprise when he told me he thought this was a fabulous idea, as he had been struggling to come up with something where the salon could "give back" to the community. I was overjoyed. When I told the head of the program, she was thrilled. It was a complete secret and when the girls arrived the following week, they were told there was a change of plans this night. We handed each girl a crown and she was told to wear it with pride because tonight they were all "queens for a night."

The girls didn't quite know what to make of this as we marched them over to Elizabeth Arden's. The salon was empty except for the staff. The manager welcomed us in and told the girls what the evening was about. As each girl chose her procedures, the level of smiles and laughter grew and we mentors were happy to sit around and watch the girls get pampered. This was truly a new experience for them all. At the end, we gave the staff their tips and we all thanked them; then rushed the girls across the street just in time to catch their bus back to the halfway house.

The following week, before we began our regular class, the girls shared about last week and what it had meant to them. It was very touching to hear all of their expressions of gratitude. Deep down inside I was so happy I had made this happen. The "dress for success" was to happen the next class. Each girl was allowed to pick several business outfits for when they actually had job interviews. All the mentors donated good business attire and all of the girls would have a great deal to choose from. All, that is, except the one girl in the class who was enormous. None of the donated clothes would have fit her.

As my good luck would have it, my partner Rick's daughter had married a German man whose family business was a plus-size women's clothing company and catalogue throughout Europe. The USA clothing distribution was run by his brother-in-law out of MD. I could not believe my good fortune when I called to introduce myself, reminded him how we'd previously met and made my request for his help. He agreed to "overnight" a box of clothing for me to bring to our event. When the box arrived, I took it unopened to the site. We opened the box at the church, one afternoon to find four brand new outfits for this girl to choose two. They were beautiful and totally appropriate for any job interview. When the day arrived all the girls were excited to choose their outfits, especially our plus-size girl. The director and I looked on with great joy. Once again I'd had the opportunity to make a real difference.

One of the mentors was a woman whose family was in the catering business. On the final day of the program her company prepared a beautiful lunch for the girls and their families. I sat with my mentee and her mother, who was filled with deep appreciation for this mentoring program and especially thanked me for being such a strong support for her daughter. All these years have passed and I still get a short handwritten note from my girl from time to time. She has an eight-year-old son as well as a job. This was truly one of those "making a difference and giving back" opportunities that I will treasure forever.

The MONA Years

My final full-time career began on June 1, 2000. I had known an executive vice-president of a large and prestigious electrical contracting company during my Energy Dezign days and based on all my PEPCO awards, I'll surmise that he saw me as a very good salesperson. I had run into him at an association luncheon and asked if his company might be interested in someone with my background and he said as a matter of fact, they were looking for someone to join their small sales staff. He set up a meeting for me to meet with my potential boss and sometime in April I drove to the Mona offices and met with every senior executive of the company. I had no idea that this was what a job interview for a salesperson would look like at Mona Electric Company. If I recall correctly, I met with at least six different men that day. It was quite an experience. Most of them asked the same questions but I didn't mind because each of them was a very professional and nice person. I met with everyone except anyone named Mona. I learned that day that Vincent "Cap" Mona was the owner of the company but he left the day-to-day operation to his comptroller. I was somewhat embarrassed that I had not done my homework. I might have gotten better knowledge about these men before my many interviews but as I later came to know them, there was not one I wouldn't have wanted to work for.

I went home that day totally exhausted from the interviews but very thankful that I'd had this opportunity. After writing a thank you note to each and every one of them, including Janet, who had welcomed me to Mona, that night I went to sleep with no anxiety, even though there had not been one hint as to any of them wanting me to work for the company. I had done my part; now it was up to them. About a week went by and I received a call from one of the people I'd interviewed with, offering me a position. I had no hesitation in accepting; I had now done my homework and I knew this would be a great company to be a part of. He wanted me to begin on the Tuesday after Memorial Day but as luck would have it, I had been called to jury duty to begin that day. He understood that I had to show up to court that day, but if not picked for a jury, I'd start on Wednesday. Being the gracious person that he was, he said that even if I was chosen for a trial, I could start with Mona the day after the jury was dismissed. We'd stay in touch. I was so appreciative that I was beginning a very good job with a really outstanding company. I was very lucky on "Jury Day," having been the fifteenth person chosen for a twelve-person jury. With twelve jurors and two alternates, I, along with every other person in the jury pool, was dismissed with the court's thanks. I picked up my twelve dollars from the jury room and headed home to prepare for my first day of work: the very next day.

Now the real fun was to begin. I jest. It was a rough beginning for me at Mona. To begin with, I had to be at the Mona office by 7:30 am. Talk about culture shock. I hadn't been on a schedule since my radio days, but everyone started their day at Mona at 7:30 am. Knowing nothing about Electric Service, Electrical Construction, Special Projects, Fire Alarm Systems, Voice/Data/Video or Security Systems, I began to question why they even hired me.

I worked with some fabulous people and my learning experience was truly "on the job." A client called the office sometime in my first couple of weeks and said they'd prefer anyone but me be their customer representative. Having done nothing wrong, I asked my boss to coach me, since I had no idea what could have happened. I cried through the coaching. He said I was sometimes too close to people's personal space and was too bold. I took his coaching very seriously: I toned down my persona, talked with a softer voice when I was with customers and hung up my suits to transition to khakis, Mona shirts and low shoes. This seemed to work quite well and I dressed this way for most of my stay at Mona Electric.

It was an interesting and frightening time in Washington and the Pentagon right after 9/11/2001. We now wore badges to identify us as Mona employees, and aside from essential workers, most buildings had fewer tenants working for days.

For me it was an eerie experience when I returned to DC on 9/12. There were absolutely no cars on the main streets. The people on the streets that day were not the usual business workers, though; they were military men with tanks and Uzis. They were there for days. One could not stop realizing the threat our city had experienced.

The next scare began when the DC Sniper began his killing streak. I was extremely nervous about driving around in my white Mona car. All of the electrician's trucks were also white. Police were stopping white trucks daily because someone had told the police that they had seen the sniper in a white truck. It was a scary time for me as I'd drive back to the office and hear sirens behind me. After the authorities finally caught the fugitives, Cap called in a counselor to meet with us. After this strenuous time I went to our HR person and said, "We need some uplifting Lunch and Learn programs." She smiled and said, "You do it." Thus began a series of coaching hours at Mona. I joined one of the executive VPs in presenting "The Seven Habits of Highly Effective People." I loved the opportunity to share some principles I'd learned along the way.

Mona was very generous to its employees. One year before New Year's, Cap sent all the Mona women to NY by bus, to see the Christmas Extravaganza with the Rockettes at Radio City Music Hall. It was a fabulous experience. Every year we had an annual holiday party as well as a summer family picnic and an opportunity to give back to the community by rehabbing a house for Christmas in April. Sue Mona, along with Representative Stenny Hoyer, had begun the Prince George's, MD Christmas in April in 1989. Over 2,400 homes of elderly, disabled and underprivileged people have been renovated. Over 81,000 volunteers and hundreds of businesses have had the opportunity to give back by participating and over $42 million dollars in real estate improvements have occurred. These were just some of the many rewards of being part of Mona.

Sue Mona, Cap's wife of 42 years, died at age 61 in 2003. Sue was only eight months younger than I, and for me personally it was as traumatic as if my best friend had left this earth. Although I only knew Sue for a short time, I felt very close to her and her loss was devastating, as I really thought she and I would grow old together. I spent all the weeks from her diagnosis to death in therapy and as my therapist said, as I cried sadly at each session, sharing my grief, "It's as though you are watching your own eminent death." As Cap grieved, so did I- quietly. This was the saddest experience in my adult life.

Fast forward several years and as they say, "God has a plan." Cap met, fell in love with and married Christina, his second soul mate. Seeing their happiness and love-well, I think Sue, along with all who know them both, are smiling at their happiness.

For the nine years that I worked for Mona Electric Group I can honestly say, "It was the best job ever."

The Cheetah, the Kids and the National Zoo

During my last two years at Mona, I had the good fortune to find a volunteer opportunity at the National Zoo. It definitely would not interfere with my work obligations, so I applied and was accepted into their volunteer program. Obviously all of us (men and women) loved zoo animals, so after training we got to choose the area of the zoo we wished to be in. Given that the zoo is open all year long, I chose an awesome INSIDE exhibit. It was designed to give children the full experience of what it was like to work at the zoo. Many school groups would come through during the school year and each child got to work in the food kitchen for the animals. There were recipes for each animal and the kids would put the ingredients together, ready for transportation to different areas of the zoo. Next came the exhibit where kids pretended to be zoo keepers and each morning they would check the habitat to make sure the animals had enough food and water. Next came the zookeeper's office, where all the daily information was stored in computers.

By far the exhibit that was the most popular was the veterinary hospital, where the children donned doctor coats and could check on animal X-rays and "fix" whatever animal they wanted to make better. There were stuffed animals in the hospital and the habitat so they were very "hands on." At the end of the exhibit tour I would sit down with the class and they would share what they had learned. It was very gratifying to see such excitement in the kids. Without fail, before the class left, the teacher would take a picture of the class with me. It was a joyful position to have. When we had these private groups, the exhibit was closed, but other than that it was open daily to the public. The preferred age of the children was between 8 and 11 years old. Every now and then a parent with younger ones came in and it was a little chaotic, but I'd leave it up to the parent to help me supervise.

A very important part of my zoo experience was to start my day with the cheetah. She was the most beautiful creature and I secretly adopted her. During zoo hours, there was always a volunteer outside her habitat, telling people who stopped to see her all the facts about cheetahs: how they were the fastest land animal, running at speeds up to 75 miles per hour. They are not good with humans, etc., thus their habitat at the zoo is quite large to keep the visitors far away from her. The zoo only had one and as I arrived early in the mornings, the cheetah, if she was outside, was all mine. I was always fascinated by her aloofness. That did not stop me from my a.m. talk with her. I'd tell her how gorgeous she was and how I hoped she'd have a great day. Silly as it was, it always put a smile on my face and was very nurturing. I loved that cheetah. Until the day I left, the National Zoo held a special place in my heart. It always will.

A PS to this story

When Rick's granddaughter was young and ready to give up her pacifier, her parents had instilled in her the idea of giving it to the baby monkeys because she was now a "big girl" and was moving on. She came to the zoo one day and with the help of the monkey zoo keeper, she gave her pacifier to the monkeys and the transference left her with pride. It was truly one of my sweetest memories of the National Zoo.

Becoming an Author

The year was 2008. I had gone back to Newport, RI to celebrate the fiftieth reunion of my high school class. I really had no interest in going to the reunion. What made me go was the opportunity to see all my girlfriends from my childhood. I had remained very close to some of them over the years, but others I had not seen in as long as seventeen years when we all went back to celebrate being fifty years old. I was very excited to see them and was not disappointed. Each one was splendid. Accomplished women with great history turned on my "juices" and when I returned to Washington, I told Rick I was going to write a book to honor them. He was very supportive and though I had no formal training in writing, I could not be stopped by such a minor thing. I began *THE NEWPORT GIRLS* at the end of that summer and wrote on the weekends.

After leaving Mona I wrote full time, with the help of the Newport girls. They sent me pictures from the Newport Daily

News (some as old as from 1957, 58 and 59). It was glorious to receive these old memories and I couldn't have imagined the enthusiasm of all the girls. When I asked, "Who would like to write something about what it was for YOU to be a Newport Girl for the book?" Eleven of them contributed. It was a grand collaboration!! Pictures of our teenage years began to arrive weekly, and I couldn't have been more excited.

To say I made every mistake that an author can is an understatement. Being a hyper "Type A" personality, I did not read everything I should have about how to handle pictures and newspaper photos for a book. After having made the photo store rich (that's a joke!!) by having all photos and newsprint made into black and white, I finally read the part about all photos had to be submitted in "greyscale", a term I was totally unfamiliar with. So everything went back and was converted to greyscale.

Item #2: Another step rather than a true mistake was I had to have every girl who wrote something for the book sign a release that the publisher required.

Item #3 was to get permission from the Newport Daily News to reprint all the photographs, although most of them were at least fifty years old. Apparently, anything reprinted that's less than 100 years old needs to acknowledge each picture as "reprinted courtesy of the Newport Daily News." This was not so much a problem as it put the book launch back by nearly a month in the end. Really no big deal, and I learned a great deal. First off,

READ EVERYTHING THAT THE PUBLISHER NEEDS. It was a good learning experience.

THE NEWPORT GIRLS took almost two years to complete and in 2010 I launched it in Newport with twelve of us Newport Girls. It was so thrilling. I guess the "first" of anything is a milestone in one's life.

Leenie, my best friend for over sixty years, had driven with me from Washington to Newport for our launch weekend. On our way back we stopped at a prominent bookstore to ask if they'd let me leave a few books for possible sale. I had about a dozen or so books left over from the launch and family and friend's sale, so instead of bringing them back to DC I'd try to leave them in Newport. There was an empty space on her "local books" table and I asked if I could autograph a few and put them in that space. She said it was okay and I got and signed them and put them on her table. As Leenie and I were looking at some of her greeting cards, the door opened and a local lady walked in the store and immediately picked up my book. I couldn't pass up the moment; I said, "May I tell you about the book? I wrote it." She smiled, said "yes" and I introduced her to Leenie (I dedicated the book to her) and gave her the Reader's Digest version of what it was about. She bought it. That was the beginning of my relationship with Island Books. The owner asked me to leave all the books I had after I signed them, and over the next year she ordered over one hundred autographed books from me. It was hardly like I was Nicholas Sparks, but it helped launch the book publicly and led to two book signings in Newport that summer. The Newport Daily News wrote a nice review of the book. I was so pleased.

When I returned home I began planning our DC launch, scheduled for September. That launch was exceedingly special, as not only did our family and friends come but some past clients and executives from Mona were there. What blew my mind was watching Cap Mona and his wife Christina walk in. They had planned a company meeting around my book party and had come from their summer home in Maine to celebrate the book. It was very humbling and I will be forever grateful.

Fast forward to 2016. *THE NEWPORT GIRLS* continues to sell. I have spoken to book clubs and participated in "Local Author events" in NC, where I now live. Our community asked me to speak at our club, and I've been to craft fairs and had book signings for three summers in a gift store where all the crafts are made by local artists. It all has been personally gratifying.

In 2013 I published my second book, *THE AFTERNOON*, a fictional romance novella about a very middle-aged woman who remembers all the men in her life until she finds the love she never knew could exist.

It's 2016 and I am writing this, my third book. I hope you are enjoying it and maybe, just maybe, you will be inspired to write something yourself.

North Carolina and New "Best Friends"

Since my friend Leenie and her husband had moved to Southport, NC in 2005, Rick and I visited yearly. Once we decided we'd like to live near the water in NC like my friend, we spent some time in 2007 looking for a home for retirement in Wilmington. Unbeknown to me, Rick had been emailing a local realtor, and knowing our budget, she began to show us homes in lovely neighborhoods. We finally found one we both liked and Rick bought it with the idea of using it as a rental until we retired.

Fast forward to August of 2010. The major economic and real estate downturn made renovating our Wilmington home unfeasible. So we began looking around the Wilmington area. On a visit to Leenie's, she told us of friends who had moved to Leland, NC, about six miles south of Wilmington, and less than twenty miles from three beaches. After visiting Brunswick Forest in Leland, we decided to build a home there.

I had already retired permanently and Rick decided he'd cut back on his work and commute periodically from NC to DC after we moved in to our new home.

We visited our home under construction two more times and moved in May of 2011.

Our beginning was very auspicious: the morning that the movers began to bring our furniture into our new home, Rick slipped on a moving mat and went head-first into our closed French doors, breaking his arm. I sent the movers back to their truck and quickly called 911. The EMS arrived very quickly and after slow preparation, Rick was loaded by stretcher into the ambulance and rushed to the hospital. I totally freaked out, as I couldn't leave the movers. Thus, Rick went alone. I was sick with guilt.

Finally the movers were complete and I rushed to the orthopedic hospital. Thank goodness, Rick had no major head damage, but his arm was another story. He had broken something major and we left that day with his arm in a plastic cast and a sling, to keep it in place. (An aside: after eleven weeks in that damn cast, he still needed surgery)

While all this unplanned drama was taking place, neighbors who had seen the moving truck and the ambulance right behind it, started knocking at our door, introducing themselves and questioning what had happened. What a way to meet the neighbors!!

About one week in, we were out at a local restaurant when a lovely couple approached us and, seeing Rick in his cast, acknowledged that they were our neighbors, three doors away from us. Lois and Dan became our first friends in our new neighborhood. As summer came, Lois introduced me to other women she had met and by the first of the year four women became my very good friends: Lois, Jean, Jeanne, and Mary Anne. Four of us formed a "games group," playing Scrabble and Rummy Cube every week. Our buddy Jean learned Mahjongg and formed her group with other women. We met Barbara through Jeanne (they had been neighbors in Rhode Island), and she became a "sub" for games whenever one of us couldn't make it. Amazing as it must sound, all the husbands liked each other too and we all share special occasions with each other when we can.

If I had to acknowledge each one of these girls for their special qualities, I'd have to say they all possess the same qualities: loving, caring and unbelievable support. Along with Leenie in Southport and Rick, my love, these girls comforted me with such love and caring during my big health event: DBS.

Mary Anne, once an Episcopal priest, has been my spiritual "rock" when I've really needed it. Jeanne makes glorious root beer floats and is a plant genius (so are Barb, Jean, and Lois). That's never been my strong suit. Lois has joined my book club and I love that we get to share this. All of these women are very creative and with their blessings I've tried to emulate them all at one time or another. Also, Lois and Mary Anne have created my addiction for homemade lemon squares and cranberry and apple pie.

As an aside, these girls love to shop. Not being my favorite thing to do, I rarely join them.

Over the years I've come to know and love many other wonderful women: Cindy, Peggy, Terri, Bunny, Susan, Rosi and Nancy are always there if we need one another. But I have to admit, the "Scrabble 4" are my best friends for life.

Rick has joined a wine group in the Cape Fear Men's group, and one of the wives, Audry, is a wonderful new friend.

I had no idea when we moved to NC that I'd find so many great women.

DBS

The year was 1981. Ronald Reagan was elected our 40th president. Walter Cronkite signed off for the CBS Evening News, America's first space shuttle was launched and actor William Holden dies.

At the age of sixty, my head started to move without my help and my hands started to shake. It was summertime and I sloughed it off and tried to ignore it. Weeks went by and I finally went to my general practitioner, who sent me off to the neurologist. After many tests he sat me down in his office and said, "I have good news and bad – which would you like to hear first?" I said, "The good news, please."

He said the good news was that I did not have Parkinson's. I would not die from this. Very good news.

The bad news was that the tremors would progressively get worse. At the time they were called Benign Essential Tremors; today they are just called Essential Tremors.

I was relieved and didn't worry about the condition. As the years went by, I could feel the impact of these tremors: I needed to drink everything through a straw. This ensured that I'd never spill whatever I was drinking; it just required being willing to live with this challenge.

Things began to change in 2015. I could no longer write by hand and this was very unacceptable. I felt very much incapacitated. Although Rick set me up with online banking, it was almost impossible to hit the computer keys without having to correct nearly every stroke.

I had been seeing a wonderful neurologist at Duke University Hospital in Durham, NC for Botox shots in the back of my head. These shots controlled the shaking of my head; there was no help available for my hands unless I had Deep Brain Stimulation (DBS). I would NEVER even consider anyone going into my brain--just too terrifying. On my last appointment of 2014 the doctor saw how severe my hand-shaking had become and said I was a perfect candidate for DBS. After listening to Rick's coaching, I agreed to see the neurosurgeon, and an appointment was made for early 2015.

We met the neurosurgeon in January. I got very excited about the procedure that he explained, and I decided the reward would far exceed the risk. We made an appointment for the surgery, for the end of March 2015. I have to admit that had Rick not been so wonderful and devoted to me, I never would have had the courage to even contemplate the possibility of DBS as a solution.

Fast forward to the day before the surgery: the pre-op tests went into the night and by the time we went to bed, I was PSYCHED!!

Surgery began so quickly the next morning, I hardly had time to think about what was happening. I do remember numbing shots into my head and a metal helmet secured onto my head to keep me from moving and to stabilize my head. I do remember thinking I looked like Hannibal Lecter in Silence of the Lambs. Rick took a picture and then lights out for me.

This surgery requires the surgeon to enter the brain from two different places in the thalamus, attach metal leads from there that run down the head and neck to what I call a "generator." The technical term is Deep Brain Stimulator, which is placed under the skin in the upper chest, above the breast. I chose the left side, as I am right handed. This device is approximately 1 ¼ inches wide and 3 inches long. They do make them smaller (maybe the size of a pacemaker, but that smaller DBS requires every day charging, where the bigger one does not). After living with the device for a little over a year, I'm not sure that it really matters which side it is placed on. After the DBS is properly in place, the leads are connected and the proper low voltage is determined.

The one totally interesting thing that occurred during the surgery was being awakened in the middle of surgery (absolutely no pain) and handed a clipboard. I was told by another doctor to take the pen he handed me, draw a concentric circle and write out my name. He held the clipboard as I drew a perfect circle and wrote my name beautifully, just the way I did thirteen years before.

I began to cry. That's the last thing I remember until I woke up in my hospital room. Apparently, that process is to assure the leads are in the correct place before they are secured and connected to the generator.

The post-op was challenging, but from the first day until today I can honestly say it was the bravest and greatest decision I have ever made. My hands shake infrequently, no straw is necessary, my head doesn't need Botox anymore and my handwriting is basically back to the way it used to be. I have the ability to change the settings on the generator (up or down as needed, by a clicker that is similar to a small TV remote) and I can manage most everything myself. There are two small mounds under my scalp (yes, they shaved my head but my hair grew back beautifully) to remind me what a life-altering event this surgery has been for my quality of life. I'm very grateful.

Playing the Ukulele, Dancing and Art

After my second book was launched in North Carolina and I had done several events, it was time for me to have some fun. I'd spent over two and a half years writing for our community as well as a regional magazine. I needed a break from writing so I decided to learn the ukulele.

At a wonderful ukulele studio in Wilmington, I joined six other older folks like me. Many of them had either played before or knew another instrument. I, on the other hand, had never held an instrument in my life. Our instructor was a charming young man, no older than forty-something, and he was an expert player, having learned as a child. His patience was remarkable. I was slow and somewhat dreadful. It was really fun, though, and I did meet some very lovely people. At my girlfriend's sixty-fifth birthday, I picked up my "uke" and stumbled through "Happy birthday to you." She was so sweet and appreciative; I was somewhat embarrassed.

I had most of these life experiences by myself. It was now time for Rick and me to share an event aside from "fine dining." We also enjoy traveling and the movies. We love to eat!!!

Ballroom dancing came next. It truly is a partners' activity. What a surprise that our instructor was eighty-seven years old. He was smooth as silk. His partner was pretty great as well. Rick and I went to our local cultural arts center and had a grand time. One of these days we will actually get out and DANCE!!!

My next solo adventure was taking up acrylic painting. For six weeks, at the same new cultural arts center, I painted like a child. As with the ukulele, everyone in the class was far more experienced than I, and they all created beautiful pictures while I painted like a novice. I still loved it.

About my First Book and the "Beach Sirens"

It was 2010 when I finished writing my first book, *THE NEWPORT GIRLS.* Five years later the book was still selling locally and it was pleasant to know people still enjoyed my personal story. A very new friend had bought and read it and asked her book club to read it. She also invited me to speak at her house to discuss the book and what it takes to self-publish, and I threw in all the mistakes I made and how much I learned. The day of the book club meeting I met seven lovely, smart and inquisitive women and it turned out to be a fun afternoon.

Somewhere into my "give and take" with these book ladies, I did an unorthodox thing: I asked if I could join their club. I'd never been part of a book club before. I didn't like the thought of someone else telling me what to read. I liked choosing my own books. I did like the notion of getting out of my comfort zone and broadening my horizons. As of this writing I've been a member for over a year, and the choices have been very diverse.

The "Beach Sirens" formed and named themselves about ten years ago. Since then members have come and gone and I, as a relatively new book club lady, have thoroughly enjoyed the experience, with more to come. My neighbor and friend Lois has since joined as well.

Buddha, Persimmons and Friendship

My new friend Sheryl is such a unique, funny and talented woman. She is the person who invited me to join the book club. Although we usually saw each other only once a month, when we all met, we got to know each other quite well when we drove together to where the other ladies lived. As we drove toward a club member's home, we always passed a monastery and said we'd visit one day (a totally new experience for both of us).

Sheryl is much younger than I and still works and teaches school. She usually has Tuesdays off. One day I called and asked if she'd like to have lunch and then visit the monastery; she said "yes", which continued to grow our friendship. The day was simply gorgeous and as we drove to the holy place, I think we both began to anticipate that something special, quiet and spiritual was about to take place.

It was not an ornate place-big though, and between beautiful tall trees. We took our shoes off as we entered an open door. We'd already missed their prayers, so it was deserted, or so we thought. We wound our way through several small, simple rooms until we arrived at the great hall. *Wow*, I thought. There was a huge green Buddha sitting straight in front of us, as well as other symbolic artifacts that were important to the monks and those in training who lived there. We were both thrilled and decided to sit down and light incense, make a donation and pray. Neither of us knew anything about the Buddhist religion, but we were obviously in a very holy space and we both experienced a very spiritual feeling. As we left the monastery we wandered into a novice who was training to be a monk. His generosity in answering all of our questions about the practice of Buddhism and the monastery left us both with a sense of the kindness and gentleness of the faith. It had been worth our visit.

On the way home we stopped at a unique shop that was both a restaurant and gift shop, as well as having interesting food for sale. There were a variety of cards and kitchen gifts. As Sheryl and I strolled the small store we both stopped at the persimmons. Neither of us had ever tasted one, and we asked the young woman behind the counter if she knew what they tasted like. She said she'd be happy to cut one up so we could taste for ourselves. We thought, *how nice,* and we watched her grab her crutch and walk slowly to the back room. I noticed that under her long skirt, something was missing: her leg. She returned and as we ate the very amazing fruit we asked her what had happened. She told us how she had a very rare disease at a very young age and the only cure was amputation. We both were amazed and inspired by her gentleness and happy spirit, given her situation. It also happened to be her twenty-fifth birthday that day and as Sheryl and I were purchasing our persimmons we burst into a harmonizing version of Happy Birthday. The young woman was completely very happy and said we had made her day.

We said goodbye and that we'd be back for lunch one day. As we continued our drive home we talked about our amazing adventure that day and we felt a deep bond having shared both experiences.

PS. Our next trip was to Myrtle Beach, SC to enjoy Lobster Fest at Red Lobster. We live over an hour away in North Carolina and this was the closest Red Lobster place to visit. I think our friendship has grown because we have shared book club and these little excursions. Another event: I hate to shop. After an awesome lunch (in a restaurant that was so dark, one could have an affair there), we "hit the outlets" and shopped, shopped, shopped.

What fun--no kidding.

One More Thing

Wherever I've lived and travelled, finding a superb breakfast place has been a priority. When I lived in MA it was Mel's Diner, a great place to start the day before going to work. For thirty-five years, at the beach in Rehoboth Beach, DE it was The Royal Treat, at least once a weekend from May through September. In VA it was Friendly's. Every morning Joe Thiesman (star Redskins quarterback in his day) used to bring his family in for breakfast. In Bethesda, MD it was a lovely little French bistro near my home.

Now that I've been in NC for five years and have tried several breakfast places, I have chosen my favorite: EZZELL'S BREAKFAST HOUSE in Wilmington. Although they are open from 5:00 am to 3:00 pm, breakfast rules the day.

The team there has been together for years and the staff of Melissa, Shelly, cashier Nicole and owner Chari know everything the "regulars" eat and drink. They are very

110

committed to all the customers but I get the feeling that the regulars are part of the family. David cooks everything except the eggs. Miss Ruby cooks the eggs (just eggs) all day long. One day I sat at the counter and watched Miss Ruby run the show, telling David what else besides eggs went with the orders. I watched them work so well together that when Ruby passed the plate with eggs on it to David, he didn't miss a beat putting all the other elements on it. Miss Ruby never broke an egg and she must have made at least twenty while I watched.

I noticed something on the white chalkboard at the side of the kitchen area. It was written in green:

"You have not lived unless you have done something for someone who can NEVER repay you."

I love this place...

The Last Word- Almost

I can't complete this adventure of life without giving thanks to Cape Fear Orthopedic Hospital in Wilmington, NC.

The events I've had there, though far less dramatic than those at Duke, have left a profound appreciation for everyone associated with it. I've had two hand surgeries and one leg event (enough for me, thank you). The doctors are superb and the volunteers are wonderful. As a result of all this greatness, I chose to join the team as a volunteer ambassador.

My job is to greet everyone who walks through the door and assist them with anything they might need. Whether it be a wheelchair for someone on the way to emergency, greeting visitors and escorting them to waiting rooms or the elevator, to smiling and saying goodbye to a patient, on their way out for good, when they are coming or going, it truly is "my hospital".

This is truly a privilege that I treasure.

Epilogue

As life continues to unfold, I feel like each day is truly a gift and I take nothing for granted. I cherish my wonderful family, who has always supported me through thick and thin. I love my girlfriends from the past and present who, as women, truly appreciate the challenges that we face, often as only women do. I adore the love of my life, who caught me at age fifty-eight and has never let go. His love, patience and understanding have allowed me to be my authentic self into middle age and for that matter, until the end.

I'd say that's A VERY GOOD LIFE... and what more is there to say?

Acknowledgements

As in any adventure, such as writing a book, I always appreciate the awesome people who graciously and generously gave of their time to read the drafts, make suggestions and critique honestly. There will never be enough "thank yous" to Rick Leeds, Leenie Dovel, Gretchen Kelly, Mary Anne Ciriello, Sheryl Keiper, Vonda from First Editing, Sarah Disbrow, Grace Gilmore, Robin Sawyer and the entire creative and production staff at iUniverse: a small but very powerful group who help create this book.

Elaine Colton lives with her partner, Rick, and their cat Barney in Leland, North Carolina. This is her third book.

Author Elaine Colton has jam packed her seventy-four years of life with awesome experiences—from the bold to the hilarious and from the daring to the wow. In *What More Is There to Say?*, she chronicles more than fifty years of stories, both personal and professional, including reinventing herself as an author at the age of sixty-eight.

From her teenage years to her sixties, this collection shares events and anecdotes that discuss what it takes to have a good life, what it takes to go where no woman has dared to go, what it takes to be brave enough to surrender to love at middle age, and what it takes to conquer one's fears.

What More Is There to Say? provides fodder for introspection. Colton hopes to inspire and propel others to complete the items on the bucket list, and she communicates it's never too late to have a variety of satisfying, enjoyable, and memorable life experiences.

www.iuniverse.com

Printed in the United States
By Bookmasters